The Lord Says:

"I WANT TO TALK TO YOU, YES YOU!"

Visions and Impressions

By Beverly A. Cholley

ISBN 978-1-60477-836-6

www.xulonpress.com

CONTENTS

Introduction vii

1. Write That Book! 13
2. I Got the Message! 21
3. Set Free from Shyness 25
4. In Perfect Step 29
5. How to Forgive 33
6. Be Ye Kind 45
7. Stay Near the Water 51
8. Nothing Is Too Difficult for God 55
9. Pride 59
10. Locked In 61
11. Unity 65
12. God Stretches Us 67
13. Shine Your Shields 73
14. Name Tags 77
15. Drawn to the Light 83

16. Heavy Burdens 87
17. Holding Her Tight 89
18. Mighty Woman and Man of God 93
19. Under Construction 99
20. Trust in the Lord 103
21. Iron and Clay 107
22. Darkness to Light 111
23. Trapped 117
24. Dead Wood 123
25. Seated in Heavenly Places 127
26. Are You Ready? 131

INTRODUCTION

The Lord told me very clearly that *He wants to talk to you!* This book was written to show you how God has talked to me over the years. These examples are intended to give you encouragement. I know many people who have experienced the leading of the Lord and have heard the voice of the Lord. God does not want you to be in the dark; He wants to be a part of your life. He loves you!

As you seek the Lord with all of your heart, He says that you will find Him. Listen for His voice! I have heard His voice in my mind; I have never heard an audible voice. Yet, in my mind, His voice is so clear that I hear it as though it were audible. I always have a strong impression that the Lord truly cares about my life. He wants you to know that He cares about you and your life too!

Many times as I talk to the Lord, He puts a vision in my mind. A vision is like looking at a television screen. It is also like looking at a picture that would take many words to describe. In my experience, the visions have been for the encouragement of others as well as for me. The concepts of the visions always line up with biblical Scripture. God will not go against His written Word, the Bible.

There are people who have prophetic visions about future events. My experience with visions and impressions has to do with daily walking and talking with the Lord. When God puts a vision in my mind, I always ask Him what it means. I do not try to figure it out with my own intellect.

The Lord wants to journey with you as you walk along your daily path. He wants to make the Bible come alive to you. He understands the flesh because He walked in the flesh. He is the only one who truly understands you. He wants fellowship with you! He wants to walk and talk with you as He walked and talked with Adam in the Garden of Eden. He wants you to know how special you are to Him. Maybe you don't feel special, but His Word proves that you are special, whether you feel it or not.

Maybe you have had a difficult life and cannot imagine why the God of the universe would want to talk to you. I challenge you to seek Him. You will not be disappointed! Maybe you think your prayers are not good enough. I assure you that if you are sincere, He will want to hear what you have to say. He knows you. Perhaps others have let you down, but God says that He will never leave you nor forsake you. Your family and friends may abandon you, but God is constantly drawing you to Him.

As I prayed about the visions and impressions shared in this book, I asked the Lord to help me to clarify them in an expanded way. I hope they give you a better understanding that God wants to communicate with you.

DEDICATION

This book is dedicated foremost to the Lord Jesus Christ, who told me to write this book. In addition, it is dedicated to my wonderful husband, Tom; our children and their spouses, Tom II and Barb, Jeff and Karen, and Susan and Chris; our grandchildren, Chelsea, Mason, Mitchell, and Jordan; as well as my extended family and friends. I would also like to offer a special thank you to my husband, Tom, and to Susan and Karen for their efforts in making this book a reality.

CHAPTER 1

WRITE THAT BOOK!

For about a year, I had an impression in my mind that I was supposed to write a book. This thought never left me, but because of the busyness of my life at the time, I put it on the back shelf of my mind. I didn't say anything to anyone because it was such a foreign concept to me. The feeling the Lord gave me was that I was supposed to share visions and impressions He had given me over a number of years. My reason for sharing is that God wants to talk to you, and I want to encourage you to listen. He wants fellowship with you. He loves you!

About a year later, after pondering and praying, I did something I had put off doing for about six years. I had an overwhelming drive to go through a stack of boxes in our basement and get rid of a lot of stuff. I came upon two boxes of notes and note-books and began deciding what to keep and what to throw away. My throwaway pile was getting pretty high when I opened a red notebook to see what I had written in it. I didn't even remember ever having a red stenographer's notebook!

Several pages into the book was a list of about twenty visions the Lord had given me during Bible studies and church and my personal prayer life. In my mind, I heard the Lord say, "I want you to write that book." He reminded me of when He fed the five thousand with five loaves of bread and two fish and how He told the disciples to gather up all the leftovers. They filled twelve baskets! I heard Him say in my mind, "You think those visions are like leftover crumbs, only to be used for that time, but those visions are Mine and need to be shared with others."

I remember praying, "Lord, if you really want me to write that book, then lead me and help me because I know absolutely nothing about writing a book or finding a publisher."

God's Word says that in the last days, old men will dream dreams and young men will see visions. There are numerous people, men and women, who dream dreams and see visions. In Acts 2:17 and Joel 2:28, the Bible says, "And it shall come to pass in the last days, saith God, I will pour out of my spirit upon all flesh; and your sons and your daughters shall prophesy and your young men shall see visions, and your old men shall dream dreams." God is no respecter of persons, so what He does for one, He will do for another (Acts 10:34). The Bible says in Galatians 3:28 that we are all one when we accept

Jesus Christ—neither male nor female, in the Spirit. He loves us and uses us equally (Rom. 2:11).

God wants to talk to you! He says that He stands at the door of your heart, and if you invite Him in, He will come in and sup with you and you with Him (Rev. 3:20). When you invite someone into your home, you have a conversation *with* him or her. That means that you both talk. God the Father sent His only Son, Jesus Christ, down to this earth to show us that He truly cares for us.

It would be considered very rude to invite a person into your home, ask him or her to sit down, and then go about your business as though the person didn't exist. It would also be considered very rude to constantly talk and never allow that person to speak. This may seem a little far-fetched, but it's sometimes what we do to God. But He wants fellowship with you and me!

There are prophecies throughout the Old Testament that predicted a Messiah was coming to reconcile all the people of the world to God. The New Testament is all about the Messiah, Jesus Christ; Emmanuel, God with us. God came down in the flesh as the Son, born of a virgin, to show us the way to eternal life. Isaiah 9:6 says, "For unto us a child is born, unto us a Son is given: and the government shall be upon His shoulder: and His name shall be called Wonderful, Counselor, The mighty God, The everlasting Father, The Prince of Peace." *The Son shall be called the everlasting Father!*

We inherited sin, down through the ages, from Adam. First Corinthians 5:22 tells us that in Adam all die, but in Christ all shall be made alive. Jesus Christ is the second Adam (Rom. 5:18–19). Because of our sinful natures, we tend to act out our sins. We need to be changed, to be "born again" (John 3:3; 1 Pet. 1:23).

There was no person holy and pure enough to cancel out our sin except Jesus Christ, who is God Himself. He took the curse of the law (Deut. 28:22) upon Himself (Gal. 3:13) and died on the cross to reconcile us to the Father. His Word says that He took our griefs and our sorrows (our sins and our diseases).

There are many Scriptures that tell us Jesus is God. John 8:58 says, "Before Abraham was I am." Matthew 1:23 refers to Emmanuel, "God with us." John 10:30 states, "I and the Father are *one*" (emphasis added). John 1:1 proclaims, "In the beginning was the Word, and the Word was with God, and the Word was God." Verse 14 of that same chapter continues with "the Word was made flesh, and dwelt among us." God came down in human form for us! Colossians 1:15 speaks of "[Christ] who is the image of the invisible God." First John 5:20 declares: "And we know that the son of God is come, and hath given us an understanding, that we may know Him that is true, and we are in Him that is true, even in his Son Jesus Christ. This is the true God, and eternal life."

Jesus could have avoided the cross, but He loves you and me so much that He wants to have a relationship with us. Because God is holy and pure, He could not free us from inherited sin without a blood sacrifice (Heb. 9:22; Matt. 26:28). We need the DNA of God Himself through Jesus Christ!

The Bible says God is a just God and will by no means clear the guilty. There must be a sacrifice. The Bible calls Jesus the Lamb of God, who takes away the sins of the world (John 1:29). If we ask God to forgive us for our sins, accept the sacrifice of what His Son, Jesus Christ, did on the cross, and invite Jesus Christ into our hearts, we become saved for eternal life in heaven. The Bible says that His blood washes us white as snow and we become new creatures in Christ. He set a standard of purity, and He loves you and me so much that He made a way for us to be pure for Him through Jesus Christ.

We must continually renew our minds because our sinful natures wrestle with our new natures. The devil has been condemned to a lake of fire, and he wants to convince God that none of us deserve eternal life. Demonic powers don't want us to live Christian lives. Ephesians 6:12 says, "For we wrestle not against flesh and blood, but against principalities, against powers, against the rulers of the darkness of this world, against spiritual wickedness in high places." We need to cast down "imaginations, and every high thing that exalteth itself against the knowledge of God," and bring "into captivity every thought to the obedience of Jesus Christ," according to 2 Corinthians 10:5.

Christ freely gave His life for us. He said, "No man takes my life from me" (John 10:18). Before He died on the cross, He said, "It is finished." At that time, God tore in half, from top to bottom, the huge, heavy veil covering the Holy of Holies. It was too thick to be torn by men. That symbolized a message from God that we could now freely enter His throne room and talk to Him (Matt. 27:51; Mark 15:38; Luke 23:45). Hebrews 4:16 says we can come boldly to the throne: "Let us therefore come boldly unto the throne of grace, that we may obtain mercy, and find grace to help in time of need."

He wants to talk to you! In Jeremiah 33:3, He says, "Call unto me, and I will answer thee, and show thee great and mighty things, which thou knowest not." If we are new creatures in Christ, that verse applies to us too.

Well, back to my writing this book. In obedience to God, I started writing down some of my visions and their interpretations. Several weeks later, my husband, Tom, and I attended an evangelistic Christian conference. On the second evening, before the message, the evangelist requested that we get into groups of five or six and just pray for one another. There were a few people in our group whom we did not know. We basically just prayed silently for each person and then sat down to hear the sermon.

The next day, before the morning session, one of the strangers from that group approached my husband. He told Tom that as he was praying for us, he thought he heard the Lord say something about a book that was to be published. He believed the Lord was saying to go ahead with the book. I found out later that this man's name was Allen and his wife's name was Janet. Up until that time, Tom was just trusting that I had heard from the Lord to write a book. Now the Lord through Allen confirmed to Tom that God truly wanted the book to be written and published.

The next day I attended a ladies' luncheon at the conference. Sitting next to me were two women I had just met, who were writing books! Only God could orchestrate that. One of the women had found a Christian publisher on the Internet. She was excited about their services and their caring attitude. I didn't ask her to, but the next day Marva handed me some printed material from that publisher. She even sent them my name, so I started getting information from them. I remembered saying, "Lord, if you want me to write this book, then please help me find a publisher because I know nothing about writing a book or finding a publisher." God was definitely leading the way for me!

CHAPTER 2

I GOT THE MESSAGE!

The Bible says we have not because we ask not. I had one prayer that was the same for many months. Finally one day I heard the Lord say in my mind, "I got the message!" He impressed on me to read the story of Mary and Martha and their brother Lazarus, who died.

Lazarus had been in the tomb for four days when Jesus finally arrived. Jesus shouted, "Lazarus, come forth!" Lazarus came out of the grave fully alive!

The Lord impressed on me in my mind, "I got the message"; then a little louder in my mind, *"I got the message";* then more softly, "I'm on my way to bring new life to your situation!" This word from God gave me the encouragement to wait on Him and His perfect timing. Many months later, my prayer was answered, and He really did bring new life to my situation. If you are waiting for an answer to your fervent prayer,

I can assure you that He got your message! It may seem late, but His timing is always perfect.

In the story of Lazarus, Mary and Martha sent a messenger to tell Jesus that their brother was very sick. Jesus was only a couple of miles away in another village. The women couldn't understand why He didn't come right away. Lazarus died, and all hope was gone. He had been in the grave for four days, but when Jesus commanded, "Lazarus, come forth!" he came out of the grave, still wrapped in his grave clothes. The miracle of Lazarus being raised from the dead was witnessed by a large crowd of people who wouldn't have been there if Jesus had come right away. Lazarus's coming forth from the grave demonstrated the awesome power of God and made it easier for the disciples to later understand that this same power raised Jesus from the grave.

God is awesome and powerful. Nothing is too difficult for Him! He expects us to pray, though. His Word says in James 4:2, "Ye have not because ye ask not." He wants us to talk to Him, and He wants to talk to you and me. He's never too busy, day or night. He sent us His Holy Spirit to indwell us, but we must ask for it. He says in Luke 11:11–13, "If a son shall ask bread of any of you that is a father, will he give him a stone? or if *he* ask a fish, will he for a fish give him a serpent? Or if he shall ask an egg, will he offer him a scorpion? If ye then, being evil, know how to give good gifts unto your children: how much more shall *your* heavenly Father give the Holy Spirit to them that ask him?" He will baptize (saturate) you in His Holy Spirit (Matt. 3:11; Acts 1:5). If you have invited Jesus into your heart, then He is there for you to ask Him to baptize you in His Holy Spirit. The same power that raised Jesus from the grave can be in you.

After Jesus was resurrected from the grave, He appeared to Mary Magdalene, who was near the open tomb. Later He appeared to the disciples in a locked upper room. The Bible says that He breathed on them (John 20:22). I believe this is when they became born again (1 Pet. 1:23; John 3:3). On the fortieth day after Jesus was resurrected, He was standing on the Mount of Olives. He told the disciples not to go and preach until He sent the Holy Spirit (the Comforter). Then, as He ascended into the clouds, they watched until they could no longer see Him. As they continued to look, an angel asked them why they stood gazing into the clouds. He told them that this same Jesus would return in the same manner in which He had gone into heaven (Acts 1:8–11).

God cannot lie. If He said He would return, then He will return! The Bible is His message to you and to me.

CHAPTER 3

SET FREE FROM SHYNESS

For as long as I could remember, I had always been a shy person. I did not like being shy, but I believed I was stuck for life with a shy personality. Shyness caused me to become easily embarrassed and wounded. A deep-seated fear of rejection was the culprit.

Once when our children were young, Tom and I attended a weekend Christian retreat. In the 1970s, the Jesus movement was in full swing, and it was popular for people to hug and say, "I love you." I avoided hugging as much as I could. My heart had love for my friends, but I was too shy to express it.

On Saturday evening after prayer, one of the retreat leaders gave me a hug and said the customary "I love you." I patted him on the back and said my customary "I appreciate you." He immediately looked up to the heavens and said, "Lord, you've got to warm this one up; she's frozen!" My answer was to admit that I was shy, but fine with my husband and family. Nothing more was said.

The next afternoon, we were all getting ready to leave the retreat and head for home. We had enjoyed some wonderful Bible studies, singing, and sharing meals together. As I was saying good-bye to someone, I noticed that the same retreat leader was hugging people and praying for them. He started walking toward me, and I realized I was backed into a corner and couldn't get away from another hug. He gave me a hug and said, "I love you." I patted him on the back and said, "I appreciate you." Then he quickly prayed, "Lord, you haven't warmed her up yet; she's still frozen!"

In an instant, God gave me a vision. I saw in my mind's eye another full-sized "me" standing in front of me. In the area of my heart, on the "me" in my visions, was a jail cell. Inside the jail cell was another little "me." The cell door was open. In my mind, I heard the Lord say, "Step out and love someone; I've set you free!" In that instant, I knew I had to obey the Lord and hug someone and say "I love you." In my heart, I knew this would be the key to being set free from shyness.

If you're a shy person, you will understand my dilemma. I felt like my shoes were full of cement, but I forced myself to walk across the room and give a hug to my friend Linda. I said, "I love you, Linda," and in that split second, the love of Jesus flowed through me and I was completely set free from my shyness. I felt the weight lift off my heart!

As I walked down the hallway in church the next day, I smiled and spoke to everybody. This may not seem like a big deal, if you're not shy, but God gave me an astounding revelation. Quietly in my spirit, He said, "They are not rejecting you." I hadn't understood until that moment that my particular shyness was due to a fear of rejection. I had lived most of my life with feelings of not measuring up to the standards of others, with feelings of inferiority.

God, our Father, the King of Kings and Lord of Lords, the beginning and the end, our Savior and Redeemer, does not reject you or me. He wants to fellowship with us. He wants to talk to you and to me! The Bible says in 2 Peter 3:9 that He is "not willing that any should perish," so He is constantly knocking on the door of your heart. He does not reject you!

The Bible says there is a way that seems right to man, but it is the way of death. Jesus said, "I am the way, the truth, and the life: no man cometh unto the Father, but by me" (John 14:6). Jesus wants to set you free too. He wants you to be free from the way of death, free to be bold for Him, and free to be all that He created you to be!

CHAPTER 4

IN PERFECT STEP

As typical parents, Tom and I always wanted the best for our three children. We took them to Sunday school and church and participated in church activities. They became born-again Christians at young ages. We taught them that God said in the book of Jeremiah that He had a plan for them, a plan for good, not for evil, to give them a future and a hope. He has a plan for you too, and it's a good plan!

We believe God's Word in Proverbs 11:21 that says "the seed of the righteous shall be delivered." Only by accepting the blood sacrifice of Jesus Christ can we be made righteous. Romans 5:18 says, "Therefore as by the offense of one, judgment came upon all men to condemnation; even so, by the righteousness of one, the free gift came upon all men unto justification of life." Every day we pray for our children, even though they are adults now and are married. We pray for their spouses and children too.

When our daughter was younger and dating, we felt unsettled about one of her boyfriends. We talked to God about it quite often, every day. One morning I was praying a strong, fervent prayer again, and the Lord put a vision in my mind. I saw my daughter dancing with Jesus. He caused me to look down at their feet, and I became aware that they were in perfect step. In my mind, I heard the Lord say, "She's in perfect step with Me." I remember saying, "Lord, I don't think she's in perfect step with You." He then impressed on me, "I know her heart deep down to the core of her being, and she is in perfect step with me."

Later that evening, I told my daughter about the vision and what God had said to me. She said she didn't think she was in perfect step either, but I assured her that if God said so, then it was true. That vision gave me the encouragement to trust God. It was several months later before my daughter finally broke off from dating that person.

God says in James 5:16, "The effectual fervent prayer of a righteous man availeth much." We don't always see our prayers answered right away, but He gives us sparks of hope along the way. If we're not watching and listening, we might miss some of the smaller sparks. I believe God does a lot of things in our lives, but unless we are paying attention, these things may seem insignificant. Ask Him to show you what He is doing in your life. You might be pleasantly surprised!

Psalm 32:8 says of the Lord, "I will instruct you." Isaiah 54:13 says, "And all thy children *shall* be taught of the Lord." The Lord taught me a great lesson two years after He showed me the vision of Susan dancing with Jesus. Little did we know that about two thousand miles away, a young man was almost ready to give up ever finding the woman who would make the right wife for him. He even told his mom that he would probably end up being a bachelor.

Soon after that declaration, he decided to look on classmates.com to just casually see if there were any former friends with whom he could communicate. When he came to Susan C., he wondered, *Could this be the same girl I knew when I was in the air force?* Six years had gone by, but curiosity overpowered him. He decided to send her an email. He wrote, "Are you the same Susan C. who was in the air force in Mountain Home, Idaho?" Of course, she recognized his name. She wrote back, "Yes, Chris, I'm the same Susan who knew you at Mountain Home." She typed, "Are you married now? Do you have children?" He emailed back, "No, I'm not married and never have been, and I have no children."

With that initial email exchange, a renewed friendship began. For over a year, there were daily phone calls and emails, as they lived over two thousand miles apart. There were also a few visits back and forth, meeting parents, family members, and friends. After a year of this, Susan and Chris fell in love and wanted a permanent relationship. They became engaged, and he moved to the same geographical location as our family. They were married a year after that.

They laugh now about how they never dated in the air force, even though they had a lot of the same friends and lived in the same dorm. Little did they know that years later they would be reunited. God knew all along they would end up together because He has a plan for our lives. Talk to Him and trust in Him, and you will be pleasantly surprised with the results!

The Lord taught me that His timetable is not always the same as my timetable. He taught me that He truly cares about our children. We cannot look at the circumstances but need to recognize the awesome power of the God we serve.

CHAPTER 5

HOW TO FORGIVE

The Lord taught me a lesson about forgiveness that literally changed my life. It happened years ago, but the principle never changes. I prayed a prayer like this: "Lord, I don't think I bind anybody, but if I do, please show me." Well, over a period of three or four weeks, He showed me negative attitudes I was carrying that I didn't even realize I had. He showed me irritation and anger and hurt in specific situations. When He revealed a negative emotional response in me, He led me to pray this prayer: "Lord, forgive me for being irritated [or whatever the emotion]. Unbind or set free [the person] from my irritation [or whatever the emotion] and help me to love [that person] even if I am right and even if that person never changes."

I had heard a teaching on Matthew 18:18: "Verily I say unto you, whatsoever ye shall bind on earth shall be bound in heaven; and whatsoever ye shall loose on earth shall be loosed in heaven." From Catherine Marshall's book *Something More,* I learned that we could bind people with our negative emotions. This Scripture from Matthew 18 can be used for other things too, but for now, we're dealing with emotions.

When I was a child, I remember my dad saying many times, "Life is not a bowl of cherries." In other words, life is not easy; it's difficult. Difficult situations can cause numerous negative emotions to arise.

Well, I had asked God to show me if I was guilty of binding anyone, and He showed me situations where my negative attitudes were binding one of my sons and my husband. There is a Scripture in Matthew 5 that tells us when we come to the altar to talk to God, if we have anything against anyone, we need to go to that brother and ask forgiveness. The Lord helped me to understand that Scripture in an expanded way.

He says in Isaiah 55:9, "For as the heavens are higher than the earth, so are my ways higher than your ways and my thoughts than your thoughts." God's ways are always better than our ways. In most cases, I felt that I was not at fault; and if there was forgiveness to be given, it was the responsibility of the other person. I now label this my "goody two shoes" attitude. But First Corinthians 3:18–20 says, "Let no man deceive himself. If any man among you seemeth to be wise in this world, let him become a fool, that he may be wise. For the wisdom of this world is foolishness with God. For it is written, He taketh the wise in their own craftiness. And again, the Lord knoweth the thoughts of the wise, that they are vain."

Soon after my prayer, my son, who was six years old at that time, came walking into the family room with grass and dirt on his feet. He tracked it all over the carpet. I yelled at him and reminded him that he had been told many times to wipe his feet before coming into the house. Immediately the Lord whispered into my mind and said, "You're angry because he tracked grass and dirt into the house; you're binding him." I was shocked! I thought I had a right to be angry.

In my mind, I said, "Okay, Lord, forgive me for being angry when my son tracked grass and dirt into the house. Unbind him from my anger, and help me to love him even when he drags grass and dirt into the house." It was a prayer of obedience to God's Word. I didn't really feel anything at the time, except shock that God knew my heart so well. I was merely obeying God's Word, which says to forgive.

We had an almost nightly ritual of drink spilling in our house by this same son. Sure enough, it wasn't long after my prayer asking God to show me who I was binding before my son spilled his drink again. Just like clockwork, I yelled at him for spilling his drink. I said, "How can you be so smart in school and do such stupid things?" The words were hardly out of my mouth when the Lord whispered again into my mind, "You're irritated because your son spilled his drink; you are binding him!" Once again I was shocked, but I said this silent prayer: "Lord, forgive me for being irritated when my son spilled his drink.

Please unbind him from my irritation, and help me to love him even when he spills his drink."

A couple of days later, he spilled his drink again, but God had miraculously changed my heart. I had total love for my son. As I cleaned up the mess, I said, "It's okay, honey. I know you didn't mean to spill your drink." I was totally peaceful. It was a wonderful feeling. He went from a daily ritual of spilling to never spilling anything ever again.

I wasn't trying to be a bad parent, but I was working too hard to make my son perfect, to protect him from the world. I didn't realize that my mean-spirited nagging was preventing my son from being what God intended him to be. My negative emotions were causing my love to fly out the window. God showed me there was no love when I was yelling at my son. I was disciplining, but not balancing it with love. I believe discipline is necessary, but not the way I was doing it.

Weeks before, in my prayer asking God to show me if I was binding anybody, I had asked Him two things. The first prayer was "Lord, I appreciate everything you've done for me. Please help me to praise you more." The second prayer was "Lord, please make my son happy. He never smiles, even though I hug him and tell him that I love him."

After hearing the Lord whisper, "You're angry, you're irritated, you are binding him up," I began to realize that I was an emotionally negative person. As I obeyed God's Word prayerfully and unbound my son, I began to almost immediately see a difference in him. He became very witty and had a fun personality. He smiled a lot. He started making me laugh. If I hadn't obeyed God's direction, I could have quenched my son's spirit; he could have become rebellious. Satan loves to work in those little areas and tear families apart. We are daily bombarded by demonic powers that would love to steal our joy. That's why we're told in the Lord's Prayer to pray "deliver us from evil"—every day!

In this same time frame of about three weeks, the Lord showed me how I was binding my husband, Tom. I would build up hurts against him. God showed me that even hurts are sin. Hurts lead to irritation, which leads to anger, which can lead to bitterness if we hold on to it. We had a good marriage; however, God wanted to make it better. He didn't mind answering my prayer for Him to show me if I was binding anyone.

My husband was a newly born-again Christian. He was excited that he had invited Jesus into his heart and finally knew for sure that he would go to heaven someday. He was overwhelmed that the Lord forgave him for his sins. He was amazed that the blood of Jesus had cleansed him from all unrighteousness. Most of all, he was excited to have a personal relationship with Jesus Christ.

My born-again experience came when I was about ten years old. Therefore, I thought I knew how a Christian should act. Ha! I began to try to mold Tom into my box, to be like me. I was quiet and shy, as God hadn't set me free yet. The problem was, Tom was an extrovert.

It was customary to stand in the church hallway after adult Sunday school and talk to one another before the church service began. During the three-week period of God's showing me how I was binding my son, Tom and I were standing in the church hallway and talking to several friends. My husband began telling some jokes and laughing—*loudly*. I believed we should be solemn in church. It didn't matter that everyone was enjoying Tom's company; I knew that on the way home I would need to set him straight on how to act in church. Ha!

On the way home, I said to Tom as nicely as I could: "You know, when you were standing outside the classroom telling jokes with our friends, you should have talked softly and not laughed so loud. You're supposed to be more solemn in the church building." Tom just answered, "Oh, I didn't know that."

In a split second, God spoke softly into my mind, "You're irritated that Tom talked too loud in church; you're binding him." I was shocked because I thought I was helping my husband to be a better Christian. Well, I had asked God to show me if I was binding anybody, so I began to pray in my mind: "Lord, please forgive me for being irritated when Tom told jokes and laughed too loudly in the church building. Unbind him from my irritation, and help me to love him even if he never changes."

About a week later, we were on our way home from shopping. When Tom turned onto our road, he did not put on his turn signal. I had learned to not complain out loud about his sometimes not using the turn signal. It was more of a quiet cold-war thing, a pet peeve. Well, even though I never opened my mouth, I noticed that he didn't use the turn signal. In an instant, the Lord spoke to my mind and said, "You're angry because he didn't use the turn signal; you're binding him!" I thought, *Oh no! I can't even have a pet peeve.* Quietly in my mind, I prayed: "Lord, please forgive me for being angry because Tom didn't use his turn signal. Unbind him from my anger, and help me to love him even if he never uses it."

I began to see that pet peeves are usually rooted in anger or irritation or even petty annoyances. I remembered sitting around in women's groups and sharing our pet peeves and laughing about them. I had thought it was harmless, but God called it sin.

As God showed me my heart, I began to develop a forgiving attitude. I even began unbinding strangers who cut me off in traffic. (God would soften my heart and give me things to pray for them.) Three months later when Tom came home from work, he took hold of both my hands and looked at me with a big smile on his face. He began to look very thoughtful and then said: "I can't explain it, but I have this deep love for you, deeper than when we were first married. I feel like our love is deeper than it's ever been." I answered him by saying, "I can explain it." With surprise on his face, he said, "You can?" I said, "Yes!" I then began to tell him everything I have told you in this chapter.

Unconditional love was the lesson God was trying to teach me. When Jesus Christ hung on the cross, He had every reason to be angry and hurt. He had been betrayed, false accusers had lied about Him, He was mocked, they pulled out His beard, they spit on Him, they hit Him on the head, and He was severely beaten. In spite of the persecution and crucifixion, Jesus said, "Father, forgive them, for they know not what they do." He was willing to go to the cross for us. He was made sin for us. As 2 Corinthians 5:21 says, "For he hath made him to be sin for us, who knew no sin; that we might be made the righteousness of God in him." He laid down His life so that we could be free from sin and have eternal life. He forgave us. His forgiveness is a free gift. We just have to repent and receive His free gift.

While praying one day and basically just thanking the Lord for helping me to have a better understanding of forgiveness and unconditional love, He gave me a vision. I saw a picture in my mind of two people chained together. Chains were wrapped around them so that they could not move. Between them, attached to the chains, was a huge lock. The lock had the type of opening that could be released only with a skeleton key. Off to the right of them, I saw Jesus standing with a huge skeleton key. On the bar of the key was the word *forgiveness*. At that moment, I heard the Lord speak into my mind. Jesus said: "I am a gentleman. If you choose to keep people bound, I will let you; but if you want to obey my Word and set them free, then I will set them free and I will set you free too!

The Bible says in Ephesians 4:26–27, "Be ye angry, and sin not: let not the sun go down upon your wrath: Neither give place to the devil." Anger can be demonstrated in many negative feelings.

Mark 11:25–26 says, "And when ye stand praying, forgive, if ye have aught against any; that your Father also which is in heaven may forgive you your trespasses. But if ye do not forgive, neither will your Father which is in heaven forgive your trespasses." *Webster's Dictionary* says that *aught* means "anything whatever" and "to any degree at all." It says that *any* means "any one or ones, some, no matter how many or what kind—any degree or extent." Webster says that *forgive* means "to give up resentment against or the desire to punish"; "to pardon, cancel, or absolve." So God's Word says that when we stand praying, we are to forgive if we have anything whatever, to any degree at all, against anyone or ones, some, no matter how many or what kind—to any degree or extent. Wow! That can be a heavy load!

Regardless of your age, I'm sure you can agree that at times life is difficult. My husband, Tom, likes to explain it this way: "We are all a product of our environment up to this very hour. We each bring something into a relationship that can cause misunderstanding. We know we should forgive, but when the attack comes, it fires us up inside. Our emotional temperature begins to soar. Society is moving toward a 'get even' mentality. Pride holds us back from forgiving or asking for forgiveness. We are told to forgive, but when we are wounded, it's hard to do. We don't always know how. We can't wait until we feel like forgiving because much unforgiveness lasts a lifetime." Do you know adults still holding child-hood hurts?

Forgiveness is a conscious decision—*not* a feeling! Obey God's Word and make the choice to unbind (set free) those you have something against. Unbinding someone is a prayer of obedience to God's Word. You won't always feel released at first, but God will go to work on your behalf. He will do one of three things: (1) change you, (2) change your situation, or (3) change the other person. You can pray something like this:

Dear Father,

Please forgive me for [the feeling or situation]. Unbind [him or her] from my judging and hampering Your work, and help me to love [him or her] even if [he or she] never changes. Please set [him or her] free from my judgment [even if I am right]. In Jesus' name, amen.

This is a prayer of obedience to God's Word. You may not feel like setting someone free. Sometimes staying mad *feels* good, but *true joy* and *freedom* come from using godly principles with promise. Matthew 18:18 gives us such a promise.

In Ephesians 4:31–32, we are told to let all bitter-ness, wrath, anger, fighting, evil speaking, and malice be put away from us. We are told to be kind to one another, tenderhearted, forgiving one another, even as God for Christ's' sake has forgiven us.

Here are some common negative, judgmental feelings: aggravated, angry, annoyed, disappointed, disgusted, dismayed, displeased, exasperated, enraged, fed up, frustrated, begrudging, full of hate, humiliated, hurt, incensed, indignant, inflamed, irritated, jealous, loathing, offended, peeved, holding pet peeves, provoked, full of rage, rejected, resentful, ticked off, and wounded.

God wants to talk to you. He wants to help you in your everyday life. He loves you more than you can ever imagine! Isaiah 40:28 says, "Hast thou not known? Hast thou not heard, *that* the everlasting God, the Lord, the Creator of the ends of the earth, fainteth not, neither is weary? *there is* no searching of his understanding."

I was on a Christian radio talk show several years ago, and beforehand I asked the Lord to give me something that He would like the listening audience to know. The Lord put a Scripture in my mind (Joel 2:25). He said, "I will restore to you the years that the locusts hath eaten."

You may think that too many years have gone by, too much damage has been done, or too much time has been wasted; but God is a God of restoration. Maybe you need to forgive someone who died years ago. Ask the Lord to forgive you for holding that negative emotion against that person, and ask Him to set you free. The good news is that the person you are setting free (unbinding) does not necessarily even have to know that you are setting him or her free.

Remember, Jesus was made to be sin for you and me. He paid our debt (2 Cor. 5:21). Trust Him to bring restoration to your life. In Jeremiah 29:11 the Lord confirms He does have a plan for your life. He says that it is a good plan, not for evil, to give you a future and a hope. God is no respecter of persons, so what He does for one, He will do for you.

CHAPTER 6

BE YE KIND

Satisfaction is not always guaranteed when you're growing up with siblings. There were six of us, and we had some pretty good times together. My brothers, Bruce and Bud, would work for hours mowing with a push mower in the farmer's field behind our house. Pretty soon they would have the baseball diamond ready for us and a few neighbor kids to play ball. I don't remember what my two youngest siblings did, but knowing how we the older siblings acted, we probably gave Byron and Belinda the privilege of chasing after the foul balls!

We used to climb the mulberry tree and pick mulberries for Mom to bake pies. We played checkers together and canasta, Clue, Monopoly, double solitaire, rummy, and many other indoor games. Outside we played hide-and-seek, kick the can, red light/green light, Simon says, and king of the hill. We went on bike rides, ice- and roller-skated, and played mumblety-peg, badminton, and anything else we could think of.

One summer Bruce made some stilts for us. We spent days walking around on them. It was total enter-tainment! Sometimes we would just sit on the porch swing. We had a lot of fun, but we could also get into some shouting matches and not speak to each other for days.

My older sister, Barbara, was my best friend. We seldom fought. She got me out of trouble one day. I don't know why Bruce had climbed out of the window and onto the roof of our house, but for some unknown reason, I was mad at him. I took off my shoe and threw it at him as hard as I could. Of course, he moved, and my shoe went right past him and broke the window. Barbara took me to her girlfriend's house until Dad had come home and cooled off a bit. That was the first time I experienced a miracle. He fixed the window and never said a word to me. That was out of character for him. Mom never said, but I'm sure she smoothed things over for me.

The point I'm trying to make is, siblings fight, even when they love one another. It wasn't until I left home for college that I realized how much time we had wasted fighting with one another. We had a lot of fun together, but we could have had more fun if we hadn't wasted time being mad. I made up my mind that if I ever got married and had children, I would help them to be friends with one another.

Everything went along fine with my three chil-dren until the two boys became teenagers. Many days they would come home from school and get into an argument with each other. After school was the worst time because they were tired, hungry, and usually had a lot of homework. When the uproar would start, I would silently pray for wisdom. I had learned from the Bible in James 1 that if I asked God for wisdom, He would give it to me freely, if I asked in faith and did not waver.

I would pray something like this: "Lord, you said in your Word that you are a very present help in times of trouble. I need your help right now. Please give me wisdom to say what I should say to these boys. In Jesus' name, amen." Always the Lord would impress on me, in my mind, a certain Scripture to tell them. I would become the mediator and say to them whatever Scripture the Lord had given to me. Most of the time they quieted down, even when they weren't happy with what I said to them. This scenario happened a few times a week for many months.

Finally, the boys grew tired of my frequent inter-ference and accused me of always preaching to them. Remember, I didn't want them wasting their years being mad at each other. After that accusation, I went to God in prayer and said: "Dear Lord, please forgive me if I've been doing things the wrong way. I don't want to preach just for the sake of preaching. I want the kids to understand your Word, but I don't want to get in the way and end up turning them against You. Please help me to raise them the way You want them raised."

I was quiet for a few minutes and then in my mind I heard the Lord say: "I told you to train up your chil-dren in the way they should go. My words are not a suggestion; it's the way they should go." Not long after that, there was another after-school argument. I did my usual praying and asking for wisdom. God did His usual and gave me Scripture to pass on to them. Again they accused me of always preaching to them.

I answered by saying: "Guys, I was concerned when you accused me of preaching to you so I talked to God about it. He said, 'I told you that you should train up your children in the way they should go. My words are not suggestions; it's the way they should go.'" I continued: "Guess what, guys? I would rather have you two mad at me than to have God mad at me." They looked surprised at my answer, but they never complained about my giving them Scripture ever again. Their frequent arguments subsided somewhat after my declaration.

One time after that, they had another after-school argument. They were yelling at each other, and I started praying again for wisdom. This time the Lord did something totally different. Immediately He put a new song in my mind, words and music! It was short but effective. Quietly, in the midst of their yelling, I began to sing these words from Jesus: "Be ye kind, one to another. Be ye kind, one to another. Be ye kind, one to another, for the Lord is kind to you." I sang it three times.

After the second time, they stopped shouting at each other and looked at me and listened. When I finished the third time, they looked at each other and then started laughing. They asked me why I was singing, and I told them that when I asked the Lord for wisdom, He gave me that song. I was as surprised as they. After that, whenever they would argue, I would just sing that same song and they would quiet down. As they became older teens and had an occasional argument, all I had to do was just say, "Okay, guys, do you want me to sing?" They would quickly answer: "No, no, don't sing. We'll stop—please don't sing!" Then they would laugh and become friends again.

Aren't God's weapons wonderful? He wants to give you His wisdom in your everyday situations. Just ask Him. He loves you and truly wants to help you! His wisdom is always so much better than our wisdom. We've laughed a lot over the years about the "be ye kind" song. For years I kept the Scripture from Ephesians 4:31–32 taped to our refrigerator door to remind the kids to be kind to one another.

CHAPTER 7

STAY NEAR THE WATER

As I was worshiping the Lord with a group of Christians, a picture popped into my mind. It was a field of bamboo growing along the water. In my mind, I heard the Lord say, "Be pliable. Stay near the water of the Holy Spirit so you can be bendable; otherwise, you will dry up and snap and break under pressure." I shared the vision with the group.

Jesus talked to a woman at Jacob's well about living water. It was about noon when Jesus was sitting near the well. A Samaritan woman came to the well to draw water. Jesus asked her for a drink. He was not thirsty; He just wanted to talk to her about spiritual things. She asked Jesus why He would ask her for a drink, since Jews had nothing to do with Samaritans. She was obviously surprised that Jesus would even talk to her. Jesus answered her question and said in John 4:10, "If thou knowest the gift of God, and who it is that saith to thee, Give me to drink; thou wouldest have asked of him, and he would have given thee living water."

The woman asked Jesus to give her this water so she would not be thirsty and would not need to draw water at the well anymore. Jesus told her to go and get her husband and then come back. She answered by saying she had no husband. He confirmed to her that, in fact, she had no husband and had actually had five husbands. He told her that the one she had now was not her husband. When He revealed these things to her, she told Him that she realized He was a prophet.

Jesus began to talk to her about spiritual matters. He said, "But the hour cometh, and now is, when the true worshippers shall worship the Father in spirit and in truth: for the Father seeketh such to worship him. God is a Spirit: and they that worship him must worship him in spirit and in truth" (John 4:23–24). The woman told Him that she knew the Messiah, called Christ, was coming. Jesus told her, "I that speak unto thee am he" (v. 26). He told her that He was the Messiah!

She was so amazed about the living water He was giving to her that she left her water pot at the well and went into the city. She said, "Come, see a man, which told me all things that ever I did: is not this the Christ?" [the Messiah] (John 4:29). Her enthusiasm was so great that many Samaritans went to the well to hear Jesus. They asked Him to stay with them for a while. He stayed for two days and continued to give them words that contained life. Then they said to the woman, "Now we believe, not because of thy saying: for we have heard him ourselves, and know that this is indeed the Christ, the Saviour of the world" (John 4:42).

This Samaritan woman was just going through her daily routine. She was probably going to the well at noon to avoid the other women who scorned her for her lifestyle. The Bible does not elaborate on the problems of this woman. Did she have children? Was she hurt, angry, abused? Did one of her husbands make her a widow at one time or another? We don't know, but Jesus knew that she needed to hear some good news. How about you? Do you need to hear some good news? Jesus is waiting for you right along the path of your daily routine. He is your salvation and your living water. Listen for His voice today, and stay near His living water. Let Him bend you into something beautiful. Stay pliable! Colossians 1:27 tells us what is the mystery of Christ. It says, "To whom God would make known what *is* the riches of the glory of this mystery among the Gentiles; which is Christ in you, the hope of glory."

In the biblical time of Christ, the Samaritans enjoyed hearing what Jesus had to say for two days, but now we can enjoy His presence twenty-four hours a day, seven days a week. When we invite Him into our hearts and ask Him to fill us with His Holy Spirit, something mysterious happens. He actually comes in! Jesus talked about this in John 17:20–26, when He prayed for those who believed and also for those who would believe in Him in the future. He finished the prayer by saying, "And I have declared unto them thy name, and will declare it: that the love wherewith thou hast loved me may be in them and I in them."

In the Old Testament book of Exodus, God instructed Moses exactly how to make Him a sanctuary, a dwelling place. He was told to make an ark out of acacia wood and to cover it with pure gold. He was told to make a mercy seat of pure gold for the top of the ark. In Exodus 25:22, the Lord said, "And there I will meet with thee, and I will commune with thee from above the mercy seat." God meets us at the mercy seat to talk with us. Now that the Holy Spirit is with us, God will meet us wherever we are; He wants to talk to you and me! Jesus is at the mercy seat waiting to commune with you, just as He was waiting to talk to the Samaritan woman at the well. Jesus is your living water. Drink of Him to satisfy your thirst (Rev. 21:6).

CHAPTER 8

NOTHING IS TOO DIFFICULT FOR GOD

One evening as I worshiped with other believers, the Lord put the following vision in my mind: I saw a square bowling ball near one of the people in the circle. I saw a hand throw the square ball. As it swiftly rolled, it became round. I had the impression that the Lord said: "Nothing is too difficult for Me! You [meaning anyone] think you can't do what I've asked you to do, but all things are possible with Me. If I ask you to do something, I will give you the ability to do it." Later a person in the group said that she knew the Lord wanted her to do something specific, but she didn't think she could. She had been asked by a church staff member to take over a certain position, but she felt incapable of handling the job. She accepted the position, while daily asking the

Lord to help her. It was only for a season, but she did an exceptional job and always gave God the glory.

Do not worry about what the Lord asks you to do because He will always give you the ability to do it. Even if your life has been broken into many pieces, He will pick up the pieces and make something useful from them. Nothing is wasted with the Lord.

Take each piece and examine it. If you don't know what you learned from each situation in your life, ask Jesus to tell you. Did you learn humility, compassion, understanding, and mercy, or are you harboring hurt, anger, and fear? If it is the latter, then ask the Lord to forgive you. Get the slate clean so you can hear the Lord tell you what you truly learned. He will take those life lessons you learned and use them for His purpose.

Many years ago, after going through a forgiving process, I began to think about my life and what I had been through up until that moment. I remember my prayer at that time. I said: "Lord, You know everything. You knew I would turn to you and become a Christian. I don't understand why I had to go through the years of having a dad who had a volatile temper, who never hugged me or spoke the 'I love you' words to me. I have a good husband and a nice family now, but why did I have to go through those hurtful and fearful years? You said in Romans 8:28 that all things work together for good to those who love You and are called according to Your purpose. You know I've forgiven my dad and understand that he had his problems, but why did I have to suffer? What good came out of that situation?"

I asked the Lord this question every day for about three weeks because I had to know how He took "all things" and worked them together for good. Finally, as I had this talk with the Lord again and again, He answered me. In my mind and heart, I heard the Lord say, "You learned to obey." He helped me to understand that we live in a sinful, fallen world. He didn't want me to go through those difficult years, but He helped me to learn the importance of obeying Him in the process. Those difficult years helped me to run to Him at a young age.

I would not be writing this book if I hadn't learned to obey. I wouldn't be free from my shyness if I hadn't learned to obey. There are numerous Scriptures in the Bible telling us to obey the voice of the Lord. The Bible also says that if you hear His voice, do not harden your heart.

Some "obeying" Scriptures are as follows: Genesis 19:5; Deuteronomy 27:10; 30:2, 8, 20; 1 Samuel 15:22; Jeremiah 7:23; 11:4, 7; 26:13; 38:20; Zechariah 6:15; John 6:65; Hebrews 3:7–8, 15; 4:7,; 1 Peter 5:29, 32.

Thank you, Lord, for being willing to take what we have and make something useful out of us. We are grateful that nothing is too difficult for You!

CHAPTER 9

PRIDE

This vision during worship showed me a huge boat situated on dry land next to several buildings. The boat was bigger than the tall buildings. I was impressed in my mind that the boat represented God's provision, Jesus Christ. I heard a voice in my mind, saying, "Get in the boat! Get in the boat!" I saw people running into various buildings, saying, "No, I love what I've built! No! I can't get in the boat!" I saw one building that was beautiful blue polished stone, like sapphire. Suddenly the boat began to move, and it knocked down all the buildings. I said in my mind, "Lord, why wouldn't people get into the boat?" He said, "It's because of their *pride!*"

Pride kept them from admitting their need for a Savior. They didn't think they needed to be saved. They were proud of their intellect and abilities. The God of the universe was the source of their intelligence, but they did not want to give Him credit for it. They were full of themselves, puffed up with pride!

This vision reminded me of Noah. The story of Noah is in the first book of the Bible, the book of Genesis. God told Noah that He was going to cause the whole earth to be flooded. The Lord saw the sins of the people everywhere, and nobody was repenting. He gave them ample time to repent and turn from their wicked ways. Noah preached righteousness (2 Pet. 2:5) and worked on constructing an ark. God gave Noah specific directions on how to build the ark. Noah obeyed and followed the instructions exactly. The people continued to ignore their Creator.

Before the flood, people lived longer. Noah was 600 years old when the flood started (Gen. 7:6) and died at 950 (Gen. 9:29). I believe the earth was beautiful, even though men had to work to keep it that way. They were proud of their gardens, proud of their flowers, and proud of their accomplishments. They were aware of the story of Adam and Eve because Adam lived to be 930 years old. They knew they should ask God to forgive them for their sins, but they stubbornly refused. The sin of pride blinded them.

CHAPTER 10

LOCKED IN

A vision of prisoners in a biblical-times, ancient boat came to me during worship. I felt we were all part of this vision, and we were all rowing. We were rowing on the bottom level of the boat, causing it to move. There were chains around our ankles so we couldn't go anywhere. We were locked in to our situation. I asked the Lord what all this meant, and He gave me the word *strength* and said to me in my mind, "What happens when you row for a long period of time?" Then He answered His own question: "You build up strength; you become strong." The impression He gave me was that as we go through various trials and there seems to be no way out, we are building up our strength (faith and trust that God will see us through our difficulties).

After sharing the vision with the Bible study group, I felt impressed to ask if anyone had anything to add. One friend said she had felt as though she were rowing during the praise and worship. They all understood that their life difficulties were helping them to build up strength.

God wants to use you to help others. In all your difficulties, you have been building up strength. God's Word in Proverbs 3:5–6 says, "Trust in the Lord with *all* thine heart; and lean *not* unto thine own understanding. In *all* thy ways acknowledge him, and he shall direct thy paths" (emphasis added). God is directing your path. Who is He having you walk by? Is it someone who is discouraged? Is it someone needing forgiveness or love or a kind word? Is it a tired spouse or friend, an irritable or unreasonable or stubborn child? Is it someone who is unfaithful or suffering? The list goes on and on. Who is He having you walk by? God's Word in James 1:22 says, "Be doers of the word and not hearers only, deceiving your own selves." Take what you've learned and use your experiences to help someone.

The Bible was "written for our learning" (Rom. 15:4). There is great encouragement in God's Word. Second Timothy 3:16 says, "All scripture is given by inspiration of God." In the midst of our distress, we can experience God's mercy. Psalm 103 tells us that God forgives, heals, redeems, satisfies, and renews us. He crowns us with loving-kindness and tender mercies. He is gracious and slow to anger. The Lord understands that we are living in a fallen world so He is willing to help us when we cry out to Him.

The Lord says in Isaiah 43:2, "When thou passest through the waters, I will be with thee; and through the rivers, they shall not overflow thee; when thou walkest through the fire, thou shalt not be burned; neither shall the flame kindle upon thee." Psalm 46:1 says, "God *is* our refuge and strength, a very present help in trouble."

If we turn to the Lord for help during our difficulties, we will surely build up strength.

CHAPTER 11

UNITY

A round wheel made of pure gold was the first
thing I saw in a vision during worship. Then I
saw a group of ladies dancing and holding onto the
wheel. In the background, others were worshiping
(men and women). The Lord spoke the word *unity*
to me. As I watched the women worshiping, the
Lord caused two to disappear. The wheel became
off balance. Within seconds they were back, and the
wheel was balanced again. The impression the Lord
gave me was that we all have been given spiritual
gifts and must learn to use them. This is what keeps
everything in balance, and we have unity.

We are each an important part of the body for the
building up of one another (Rom. 12:4–5). It is important to gather together. Hebrews 10:25 instructs us
not to forsake the assembling of ourselves together.
Once we are part of the body of Christ, the Lord

gives us gifts to help serve one another (Rom. 12:6–15). Some gifts are prophecy, ministry, exhortation, teaching, giving, cheerful mercy and hospitality. Other spiritual gifts are listed in 1 Corinthians 12. They are the word of wisdom, the word of knowledge, faith, gifts of healing, working of miracles, discerning of spirits, various kinds of tongues, and interpretation of tongues.

We are all part of the same body, with one Spirit, but we have a variety of gifts. This is explained extensively in 1 Corinthians 12. We are all the body of Christ. Above all the gifts is love. If we do not have love, the Bible says we are nothing (1 Cor. 13:2).

Unity is extremely important to the Lord. God is not the author of confusion. He is organized and wants us to be unified with Him.

CHAPTER 12

GOD STRETCHES US

As we were worshiping at church on a Wednesday evening, the Lord showed me a vision. I saw the pastor walk up the walls, across the ceiling, and down the other side of the wall. He walked to the front of the sanctuary and began to do jumping jacks and run in place. Then he stretched his arms out horizontally and kept saying, "Stretch... stretch... stretch!" I felt like the Lord had been and was and would be using this pastor to cause the congregation to think and do beyond their natural abilities.

The word the Lord gave me was "My ways are higher than your ways; My thoughts are higher than your thoughts." I believe the Lord is going to do more than we would expect in the natural and that we should be looking for greater things to happen. I had the feeling of excitement. The pastor's face had a big grin, and he seemed to be full of joy, peace, and excitement. He seemed confident in the Lord's leading.

Do you ever feel like you're being stretched? Have you ever been forced to think outside the box? Has your faith been stretched more and more? God has more for you if you will trust Him and listen for His voice.

Picture a baby being encouraged to stand up and then to take a few steps. Pretty soon the baby is toddling along and eventually walking with confidence. All along, the baby is growing and getting stronger and understanding more and more. God does not want us to stay in the cradle. He wants us to walk and talk with Him and learn from Him.

God will not mislead you. Hebrews 6:18 says, "in which *it was* impossible for God to lie." Numbers 23:19 says, "God *is* not a man, that he should lie." If He says that He will teach us, then He will (John 14:26)!

When the baby is no longer a toddler and has learned to run, play, and carry on a suitable conversation, the parents push him or her further. Now they say, "It's time for you to leave the house for a while and go to school." They want the child to learn more, so the child must leave the comfort zone and go to school, where possibly he or she does not know anybody. I remember leaving my comfort zone and walking to school. I cried on my first day of school because I didn't know what to expect. I was afraid. It did not seem fair that I couldn't have Mom with me. She was my comfort.

The fascinating part of being a born-again Christian is that we don't have to leave our comfort zone. Jesus Christ promised to send us the Holy Spirit, also called the Holy Ghost, or the Comforter. The Bible gives us the words of Jesus concerning this in John 14:15–20 (emphasis added):

If ye love me, keep my commandments. And I will pray the Father, and he shall give you another comforter, that he may abide with you for ever; even the Spirit of truth; whom the world cannot receive, because it seeth him not, neither knoweth him: but ye know him; for he dwelleth *with* you, and shall be in you. I will not leave you comfortless: I will come to you. Yet a little while and the world seeth Me no more; but ye see Me: because I live, ye shall live also. At that day ye shall know that I am in My Father and ye in Me and I in you.

John the Baptist preached about the Holy Ghost in Matthew 3:11. He said, "I indeed baptize you with water unto repentance: but He that cometh after me is mightier than I, whose shoes I am not worthy to bear; he shall baptize you with the Holy Ghost and with fire." If you are going to be stretched, you need the power of the Holy Spirit in your life. The Comforter will go with you wherever you go!

Jesus taught about living outside the box. Our natural instincts would not permit us to do some of the things He taught. In the book of Matthew, He says to turn the other cheek, go the extra mile, love the unlovable, love your enemies, bless those who curse you, do good to those who hate you, pray for those who despitefully use you, and pray for those who persecute you. God's Word tells us to rejoice when we are being persecuted because of Christ (1 Pet. 4:12–14).

After teaching the disciples how to pray by giving them the example of the Lord's Prayer, Jesus instructed them on the importance of forgiving. He said in Matthew 6:14–15, "For if ye forgive men their trespasses, your heavenly Father will also forgive you: but if ye forgive not men their trespasses, neither will your Father forgive your trespasses."

When I was in grade school, I would walk home most days with a couple of my friends. At least once or twice a month, one of the school bullies would chase us and threaten to hit us. We were always able to outrun him, but there was a lot of fear of the unknown in our hearts. After this had happened for over a year, the Lord taught me an interesting lesson. In Sunday school, we were taught how the Bible tells us to love our enemies. Jerusalem was being governed by Rome during the time that Jesus was preaching and teaching. The Roman soldiers had the authority to require people to carry their heavy packs, but only for one mile. Jesus told the Jewish people to go two miles for whoever compelled them to go one mile. I remember thinking how cruel those Roman soldiers must have been. I thought it would be so hard to do good to those who hate you. The concept baffled me. I thought about it for weeks!

One summer day I walked by myself to the candy store, which was about one mile from my house. It was actually a gas station that had a glass case full of penny candy, back when you could buy a piece of candy for a penny. What a delight it was to pick out eight pieces of candy! The biggest piece I bought that day cost me three cents, and I was looking forward to eating it. Just the thought of it made me so happy. As I walked across the station lot, I glanced across the side road and there stood "the bully"! In an instant, I went from happiness to doom and gloom. He was staring right at me. I was sure that he saw my small brown bag containing my treasured candy.

Panic arose in my heart, but at the same time, an idea sprouted in my mind. The Lord reminded me of my Sunday school lesson to go the extra mile, to do good to those who hate you. Immediately I knew what to do. I put on my biggest smile and called him over to where I was standing. I said, "Would you like a piece of my candy?" His countenance changed from gruff to bewilderment. He said, "Yes." I held my bag toward him, and he reached in and took my best piece of candy. Then he walked away in disbelief.

Now you might say, "What a brat; he took your best piece of candy!" My perspective was different. I was amazed that he did not chase me and hit me and take my whole bag of candy! I was also amazed at God's wisdom. Later in the school year, I saw that boy only one more time, from a distance on the playground. I was never bullied again. He must have eventually moved away because I never saw him after that last time.

Don't be surprised if you feel as though you are being stretched sometimes. That would be a good time to call on the Lord and to trust Him with the directions He gives to you.

CHAPTER 13

SHINE YOUR SHIELDS

A pile of dirty shields came to my mind's eye as I worshiped the Lord with others before our Bible study began. In my heart, I knew we were to pick up our shields. In my mind, I heard the Lord say, "Shine your shields!" The shield represents our faith. "Now faith is the substance of things hoped for, the evidence of things not seen" (Heb. 11:1). I shared this with the group.

The Lord wants us to look at the truth of His Word, not at our circumstances. When we focus on the storms around us, we are not exercising our faith in what God can do. He says that we are more than conquerors (Rom. 8:37). He gives us a sound mind, not a spirit of fear (2 Tim. 1:7).

I was talking with a young mother one day and listening to what she had to share. I was also silently asking the Lord to give me wisdom to encourage her.

In my mind, I heard the Lord say, "She is bottled-up wisdom." I saw a jar that was expanding, even though in the natural, it would not be capable of doing so without breaking. I saw the lid come off the jar. The Lord had been teaching her many things during her daily situations of raising children. She had much wisdom to offer others, and her faith level was rising. She understood that God was faithful, because she had been calling on Him for help for many years. In the midst of her difficult life, though, she did not realize that she was storing up wisdom to share and that her faith would encourage others.

"Without faith it is impossible to please him: for he that cometh to God must believe that he is, and that he is a rewarder of them that diligently seek him" (Heb. 11:6). The Bible says in Ephesians 6:16, "Above all, taking the shield of faith, wherewith ye shall be able to quench all the fiery darts of the wicked."

Paul, who was called to preach by the Lord Himself, used the example of the Roman soldier's equipment to describe the Christian's spiritual equipment. He compared the Christian's faith to the soldier's shield. He called our faith a shield of faith. When we hear in our minds the enemy trying to defeat us with lies and deception, we need to hold up our faith shields to stop those darts. We must say, "No, God's Word is true!" We must talk to God and ask Him to show us His perspective on our situation and ask Him to help us. He is faithful!

Matthew 17:20 compares our faith to a mustard seed. A mustard seed is very small; it's tiny.

Nevertheless, that amount of faith is enough to move mountains. Even though a mustard seed is the smallest seed, it produces a very large plant. Our seed of faith can plow right through the mountain of doubt. The seed of faith may start out small, but as it rolls, it becomes bigger and bigger until it finally overwhelms the doubt.

If you mix certain ingredients together in a bowl, put the mixture in a pan, and then bake it, you already know what the end result will be. If you mix your seed of faith with the truth of God's Word, believe His Word, and act on His Word, you will have victorious results.

Faith without works is dead according to James 2:17, 20, and 26. You can put three or four bowls on your countertop and put precise ingredients into each bowl. Each bowl will contain the ingredients for a specific recipe. You can admire each container. You might even say, "Wow, this one is going to be a cake, this one is going to be brownies, that other one is going to be banana nut bread," and so on. You can believe it with all your heart, but until you act on it by putting those mixtures into pans and baking them in the oven, you will not see the finished cake, brownies, and banana nut bread.

Acting on your faith can be helping someone in need, making a phone call, sending a note or card or email, praying with someone, or whatever else you believe the Lord wants you to do. The shield of faith says: "I'm going to listen to God and hold up this shield in the face of adversity. I'm going to act on God's Word."

The Lord expects our faith to go beyond the church doors and into our everyday lives. Our salvation is free in Christ Jesus, but the Lord wants us to walk in good works because we are saved (Eph. 2:8–10). This means to put on a smile and do your very best at work, to help a coworker who may be facing a challenging day, to avoid complaining, and to be honest and trustworthy. It means being kind and gracious and forgiving. Sometimes a mistake can be turned into a teaching moment rather than a rebuke.

Yes, the Lord wants us to shine our shields and walk in faith. It's easier to walk in faith if we are in communication with the Lord and looking for His return. Hebrews 12:2 tells us to look to Jesus, the author and finisher of our faith. He wants to help you with your daily life. He wants to talk to you.

CHAPTER 14

NAME TAGS

In church during worship, the Lord gave me a vision of everyone with name tags on their clothing. Some of the name tags read, "I can't," "Not my personality," "Too hard," "Too shy," "I'm discouraged," "I'm depressed," "I'm not good enough," "I'm a failure," "I'm afraid," and all kinds of other negative statements. In my mind, I heard the Lord say: "I haven't given them those name tags! My name tag for everyone is 'I can do all things through Jesus Christ who gives me strength.' " I told this to the congregation to give them encouragement.

It does not matter who you are or what you have done. God can transform you if you will let Him. You have talents and abilities that you may not even be aware of at this time. Ask Him to tell you what He has placed into you. Isaiah 64:8 says, "But now, O Lord, thou *art* our father; we *are* the clay, and thou our potter; and we all *are* the work of thy hand." The potter molds the clay. He has something specific in mind for your life. Even if you have gone your own way, you can come back to the Father. He can add the water of the Holy Spirit and change you into a beautiful, useful vessel.

Clearly we would not normally go about our daily routines with negative name tags announcing what is really inside of us. The exciting thing is that God knows what is deep in us, and He wants to change our name tags! Jeremiah 17:10 says, "I the Lord search the heart." First Chronicles 28:9 says, "for the Lord searcheth all hearts, and understandeth all the imaginations of the thoughts." In Psalm 139:1–4, King David said: "Oh Lord, thou hast searched me and known me. Thou knowest my downsitting and mine uprising; thou understandeth my thoughts afar off. Thou compassest my path and my lying down, and art acquainted with all my ways. For there is not a word in my tongue but lo, oh Lord, thou knowest it altogether."

In the book of Exodus, Moses could have worn a name tag that read, "They will not believe me" or "They will not hearken unto my voice" or "I am slow of speech." He was called by God to lead the Israelites out of the land of Egypt where they were slaves. Even after God did many miracles to convince Moses that his assignment was possible with God's help, Moses still asked Him to send somebody else. The apprehension of Moses angered the Lord (Exod. 4:14). Even so, God brought Aaron, Moses' brother, into the picture. Aaron became the spokesman for

Moses as God taught Moses what to do. God did not give up on Moses, and He will not give up on you either. He has a victorious name tag for you!

Christopher Columbus would never have discovered America if he had worn the name tag called "rejected" that people were trying to attach to him. Before setting sail, He was rejected three times and then made to wait four years. Those four years ended with more rejection. He finally set sail, but during the voyage, he experienced doubt and disappointment. His name tag "discouraged" was waiting for him on the deck of the *Santa Maria,* but before he could pick it up, land was sighted. A new world had been discovered!

Paul, a New Testament missionary, was apprehended by Jesus Christ on the road to Damascus. Prior to his encounter, Paul's name tag was "Saul, persecutor of Christians." Saul, who later became Paul, had been the overseer at Stephen's stoning for preaching about Jesus Christ. Paul gives his testimony many times throughout the Bible about how Jesus appeared to him in a bright light. The power of the Lord was so strong that Paul and his companions fell to the ground (see Acts 9:1–19).

Furthermore, Paul said:

> I heard a voice speaking unto me in the Hebrew tongue: Saul, Saul, why persecutest thou me? It is hard for thee to kick against the pricks. And I said, who art thou Lord? And he said: I am Jesus whom thou persecutest.

79

But rise and stand upon thy feet; for I have appeared unto thee for this purpose to make thee a minister and a witness both of these things which thou hast seen and of those things in the which I will appear unto thee: delivering thee from the people and from the Gentiles, unto whom now I send thee, to open their eyes and to turn them from darkness to light and from the power of Satan unto God, that they may receive forgiveness of sins and inheritance among them which are sanctified by faith that is in me.

Acts 26:14–18

When Saul stood up, his eyes were blind. He had to be led into Damascus where he prayed and did not eat for three days. The Lord sent Ananias to pray for Saul to receive his sight and to be filled with the Holy Ghost. When the scales fell from Saul's eyes, he immediately arose and was baptized.

Saul's (Paul's) new name tag could have been "Sold out to Jesus, the Messiah" or "I'm on fire for the Lord." Paul wrote about his feelings to Timothy in 1 Timothy 1:12–15: "And I thank Christ Jesus our Lord, who hath enabled me, for that he counted me faithful, putting me into the ministry; who was before a blasphemer, and a persecutor, and injurious: but I obtained mercy because I did it ignorantly in unbelief. And the grace of our Lord was exceeding abundant with faith and love which is in Christ Jesus. This is a faithful saying, and worthy of all acceptation, that Christ Jesus came into the world to save sinners *of whom I am chief"* (emphasis added).

In an earlier chapter, I told you how the Lord literally set me free from shyness. My name tag had been "I'm too shy" and "I fear rejection." Over the years, I have experienced the faithfulness of God and trust Him to always be there for me. He wants to help you too. Ask Him to give you a new name tag.

CHAPTER 15

DRAWN TO THE LIGHT

One evening during praise and worship, the Lord presented me with a vision of a gigantic chasm as big as the Grand Canyon. There was a long bridge over it, but it was covered by a pitch-black, cloud-like haze. There were no sides to the bridge, and the bridge area was so black that you could not see to get across. The born-again Christians were illuminated with light, but the black area was filled with millions of people groping around in the dark.

I had the feeling that the bridge area repre-sented life on the earth. If people chose to follow the light, they could travel across safely. The safe area on the other side represented eternity. The light of Jesus in the Christians was keeping everyone who followed it from falling into the deep canyon and being destroyed. The word of the Lord to me was John 3:16–17: "For God so loved the world that he gave his only begotten Son, that whosoever believeth in him should not perish, but have everlasting life. For God sent not his Son into the world to condemn the world; but that the world through him might be saved."

The Bible says that Jesus is the light and He lights our path. "Then spake Jesus again unto them saying, I am the light of the world; he that followeth me shall not walk in darkness but shall have the light of life" (John 8:12). "Thy word is a lamp unto my feet and a light unto my path" (Ps. 119:105). "Ye are the light of the world. A city that is set on a hill cannot be hid. Neither do men light a candle and put it under a bushel, but on a candlestick; and it giveth light unto all that are in the house. Let your light so shine before men, that they may see your good works, and glorify your Father which is in heaven" (Matt. 5:14–16). "For God who commanded the light to shine out of darkness, hath shined in our hearts, to give the light of the knowledge of the glory of God in the face of Jesus Christ" (2 Cor. 4:6). "For ye were sometimes darkness, but now are ye light in the Lord; walk as children of light" (Eph. 5:8).

Light dispels darkness. You cannot see in the dark unless you have some sort of light. God created physical light for us on the first day of creation (Gen. 1:3–5). (The Lord told a friend of mine, Glen, that true darkness is really darker than we could ever know!) On the fourth day of creation, He made the sun to rule the day and the moon to rule the night.

Man has always tried to create ways to extend the daylight hours: from torches to candles to oil lamps to electricity to daylight saving time. It is difficult to work or play in total darkness. Physical light draws people to it. Some examples are a beautiful sunrise, a colorful sunset, an airplane moving along in the night sky with all its lights glowing, a beacon of light announcing a grand opening, an oasis of light directing you to a place where you can fill up with gas or purchase a snack in the middle of the night when you are traveling, lights in the sky showing that you are approaching a city, a light on the front porch welcoming you home, a campfire giving you warmth and comfort, or a lighthouse warning of dangerous rocks or announcing a safe passageway.

It makes sense that the Lord would use light to describe Himself. Spiritually, we are being drawn to the light of Jesus. Jesus said in John 12:32, "And I, if I be lifted up from the earth, will draw all *men* unto me." He said in John 6:44, "No man can come to me, except the Father which hath sent me draw him; and I will raise him up at the last day." Second Peter 3:9–10, says, "The Lord is not slack concerning his promise, as some men count slackness, but is long-suffering to us-ward, not willing that any should perish, but that all should come to repentance. But the day of the Lord will come as a thief in the night."

Jesus wants to talk to you. In the Christian community, Christ Jesus has been compared to a lighthouse. A lighthouse is constructed on a heavy, solid rock foundation. There is an old hymn that says, "On Christ the solid rock I stand / All other ground is sinking sand / All other ground is sinking sand" ("My Hope Is Built" by Edward Mote and William

B. Bradbury). The Bible calls Jesus Christ the spiritual rock in 1 Corinthians 10:4. In Isaiah 28:16, the Lord says, "Behold, I lay in Zion for a foundation a stone, a tried stone, a precious corner stone, a sure foundation: he that believeth shall not make haste." This is a prophecy about Jesus Christ, our Messiah. When you turn to Jesus, you will be on a solid foundation and your darkness will turn to light.

CHAPTER 16

HEAVY BURDENS

One time I was feeling very overwhelmed with some difficult situations in my life. The burdens were weighing me down, and I could see no solution. Have you ever been there? I began to thank the Lord for who He is and what all He has done for me. I poured my heart out and then said: "Lord, you said in your Word that your yoke was easy and your burden was light. I'm giving you my heavy burden; I want and need your easy yoke." I stopped for a minute and then said: "Lord, you could show me if you wanted to. What is your easy yoke?" In a flash, He showed me. In my mind's eye, I saw a feather in the air above my left shoulder and a feather in the air above my right shoulder. Each feather floated down and rested on my left and right shoulders. In an instant in my mind, I heard the Lord say, "That's my easy yoke!" He wants us to wear His yoke (Matt. 11:29–30).

After giving my heavy burden to the Lord, I received a phone call from someone wanting to help me. Everything fell into place and the difficulty melted away.

Jesus is our king and high priest (Zech. 6:13). He shed His blood for us. Romans 8:34 says that Jesus makes intercession for us. He is praying for us every day (Heb. 4:15–16). He does not have stressful days, for He is God and understands the whole life picture. We have stressful days. Jesus walked in the flesh and He understands the flesh. He can relate to our problems. He wants to relate to you! Share your burdens with Him and give Him a chance to help you.

In Hebrews 9:11–13, we find that Christ was offered *once* to bear our sins. No more does the high priest have to go into the Holy of Holies once a year. The Bible says that Jesus has made atonement for our sins, not just for us but for the whole world (Rom. 5:8, 11). Thank you, Lord, for Your kindness, Your compassion, Your easy yoke, Your mercy, and Your free gift of eternal life!

CHAPTER 17

HOLDING HER TIGHT

During the music one Sunday morning, I was singing praises to the Lord along with everyone else. I prayed a heartfelt prayer for my daughter, who was in basic training in the military at that time. It was a mother's prayer for help and protection for her. She was not an athletic person, so I was concerned about her getting through basic. As I finished my short but earnest prayer, I heard in my mind the Lord say, "I'm holding her tight!" At the same time, I felt an arm around my back and a hand on my waist. I opened my eyes to see who had put their arm around me, but there was nobody there. I knew in my heart that the Lord was talking to me, and He wants to talk to you too!

I have heard people say they do not pray because they believe God is too busy with bigger problems than theirs. There is no limit to God's ability and

His willingness to help. He says that if we truly seek Him with all of our hearts, we will find Him. That's a promise!

In John 20:11–17, Mary Magdalene was standing outside the tomb where they had placed the body of Jesus after He was crucified. It was the third day. The stone had been rolled away, and the tomb was empty. Mary began to weep with overwhelming grief.

There was a man nearby who Mary assumed was the gardener. The man said to her, "Why are you weeping?" She explained that they had taken her teacher, Jesus, out of the tomb, and she did not know where they had taken Him. The man answered, "Mary." Instantly she knew it was Jesus!

I cannot even imagine how excited she must have been. He told her not to touch (don't delay) Him because He had not yet ascended to the Father. He was the sacrificial Lamb of God and had to present Himself into the heavenly Holy of Holies for all of us. Even though He needed to go quickly, His compassion for a weeping, grieving person caused Him to allow Mary to see Him. He wanted to give her encouragement. He wants to give encouragement to you too. He will take time for you, day or night, whenever you call on Him. He is totally interested in your life!

When I heard the Lord say, "I'm holding her tight" and felt His arm around me, I experienced overwhelming peace and joy. He wanted me to know that when my daughter was running in the early morning hours, He was right there with her. When she was sweating through all the required calisthenics,

He was there beside her. When she was standing at attention, at ease, eating, or sleeping, He was there watching over her.

There was one prayer that Tom and I prayed over and over. We asked the Lord to give her favor and hide her from the harassment of the drill instructor. It was an endurance test for Susan! On the day of her graduation, her drill sergeant described each airman in Susan's squadron of thirty-eight girls before handing them their completion certificate. The drill instructor's description of Susan was "This is an airman who somehow managed to *never* get a 341 [similar to a demerit and easy to get]; and also, I don't know how, but she managed to remain *invisible* during basic training." God's answer: *favor* and *invisibility!* Isn't that awesome? We serve a mighty God who is very able to answer prayers. Draw near to Him and listen for His voice.

CHAPTER 18

MIGHTY WOMAN AND MAN OF GOD

While I was in a meeting with a few women at church, one friend shared that she was feeling depressed and did not feel as though her life was making any difference to anyone. Of course, that was not true, but she still had those heavy feelings. We decided to pray for her. In the course of the prayer, a vision came into my mind. I saw the ocean with a very beautiful ornate ship that was stuck on a sandbar. I saw Jesus standing next to the ship, with His hands on the bow of the ship. It did not make sense to me, so in my mind I said, "Lord, what are you doing?" He answered, "I'm pushing this mighty woman of God off this sandbar." I said to this friend, "God just called you a mighty woman of God!" You may think you don't matter, but He calls you mighty! This friend had been a Christian for many years, born again and filled with the Holy Spirit. Even so, she was stuck temporarily and could not see her situation from God's perspective. The Lord was there to give her a spiritual boost.

This reminds me of Gideon. God called him a mighty man of valor when he was hiding from the enemy, the Midianites. Gideon was threshing wheat by the winepress and hiding it so the Midianites would not find it. The Midianites had already destroyed the Israelites' crops and left no food for Israel. The people were in poverty. "And the angel of the Lord appeared unto him, and said unto him, The Lord is with thee, thou mighty man of valor" (Judg. 6:12).

The Lord proceeded to have many conversations with Gideon. Gideon gained confidence as he followed the Lord's specific instructions. The Lord used Gideon to rescue the Israelites from the Midianites. The first task given to Gideon by the Lord was to destroy all the idols that the Israelites were worshiping.

The Lord did not want the Israelites to take credit for the victory, so He reduced Gideon's army from thirty-two thousand to only three hundred men. Gideon was apprehensive, but God gave him strong encouragement when He sent Gideon and his servant, Phurah, down to the enemy's camp at night. The Lord allowed them to overhear a conversation between a man and his fellow soldier.

The man told of a dream he had about a cake of barley bread that tumbled into the camp and knocked a tent down flat. Judges 7:14 says, "And his fellow answered and said, This is nothing else save the sword of Gideon the son of Joash, a man of Israel: for into his hand hath God delivered Midian and all the host [camp]." When Gideon heard the telling of the dream and the interpretation, he worshiped God and returned to his army. He was now confident that the Lord was going to give them victory.

Before that, Gideon felt inferior, like a loser. He was apprehensive and felt like the least person for God to choose. He did not feel like a mighty man of valor. He had not been looking at his circumstances from God's perspective. But He became a mighty man of valor because of God's help and God's instructions.

Gideon divided his three hundred men into three companies. He put a trumpet into every man's hand. Each man also had a pitcher with a torch inside. They surrounded the Midianite camp that night. When Gideon blew his trumpet, they all blew their trumpets, broke their pitchers, and held their torches with one hand and continued to blow their trumpets. They all shouted, "The sword of the Lord and of Gideon!" This caused mass confusion in the camp so that the Midianite soldiers began to fight one another with their swords, and those who were not killed fled to other cities. Eventually all were captured, and there was peace for forty years.

The Lord wants to be involved in your life. Talk to Him, and listen to what He has to say to you. Be obedient. God's ways are always the best ways!

I want to talk to you about the three hundred men God chose to be a part of Gideon's army. Even though their names are not in the Bible, I believe they made a great impact on their families and friends and even people who did not know them before the battle. Can you imagine their excitement when the plan worked? Certainly their intoxicating joy spilled over into the whole community. They had experienced the wisdom and the awesomeness of God. They had seen God outwit the enemy. They finally understood the paramount importance of having God on their side.

What a celebration they must have had! I'm sure their worship of God was enthusiastic. God had set them free from the oppression of the enemy. Along with Gideon, they were all witnesses of God's glorious triumph. People were looking at them and listening to them tell the story, telling their experience!

The Bible says in 2 Corinthians 3:2 that our lives are like written letters: "Ye are our epistle written in our hearts, known and read of all men." Our lives are open books (good or bad), never closed but always open. No matter who you are, your life is being read every day. What do you want people to read? What do you want those closest to you to read? Maybe you want God to erase some of the words you have written. He does that when you repent and ask His forgiveness and ask Him to cleanse you (1 John 1:9). He is faithful.

Victory is what the Lord wants for you and me. Do not listen to the lies of the enemy. Read and study God's Word; He is for you, not against you! The enemy comes to steal, kill, and destroy, but Jesus came to give us life and to give that life more abundantly.

My "mighty woman of God" friend has experienced some difficult times, but through them God has made her stronger and more victorious. She is the kind of person I would go to for prayer because she understands that God is always faithful. Her life is an open book, and people are reading that she is trustworthy and compassionate and truly loves the Lord.

We should all want the characteristics of Jesus Christ to be written in us and to be read by all men. We are all mighty when we listen to the Lord and obey Him. He wants to talk to you, fellowship with you, and hear from you.

CHAPTER 19

UNDER CONSTRUCTION

During worship I was given a vision of a house under construction. My impression from the Lord was "God is at work in us, helping us to do right. He has begun a good work in us, and *He will finish it.*" The Scripture for this is found in Philippians 1:6: "Being confident of this very thing, that he which hath begun a good work in you will perform it until the day of Jesus Christ." I shared this with the church home group.

If you can picture yourself as a house being built, then you can understand the parallel of God doing the spiritual building. First, the builder must get a permit to build. That would be when you turn your life over to the Lord by repenting of your sins and believing on the sacrifice of Jesus on the cross for your sins. You believe that you have eternal life because of His blood.

Second, the builder meets with the customer to decide on the plan for the home and all the contents, right down to the color of paint and types of faucets. This is the happy spiritual state of realizing that God is for you and you have His daily help and promises. You begin to understand that heaven is your destiny, and things are looking good. You can already picture the beautiful house.

Third, the foundation is put into place, and structure starts to rise out of the ground. This is when everyday life sets in, and occasionally, like a builder, you have some difficult times, such as dealing with a nail gun here, a hammer there, some sawing, some pounding, some wiring, heating and cooling, hanging doors, insulating, and so forth. The Lord starts to hit you with His Word to clean up, straighten up, listen, trust, and obey. There are doors you can't go through anymore because they would take you back to your sinful years. Some days you may wonder if being a Christian is worth it at all; you may be hot one day and cold the next. Even so, you understand that He loves you enough to want to do a good work in you.

The roof goes on, and you now realize that you must renew your mind and put on the mind of Christ. The work has begun, so you must protect what comes into your house (Rom. 12:2; 1 Cor. 2:16). The outside of the house is insulated and protected by a covering of siding, brick, wood, stucco, or stone. Spiritually, this could be God's protection on what comes in to you (the house). Then the house is wired, up and down and around. The wiring could represent the Holy Spirit being everywhere with easy accessibility.

You tell the builder that you want plenty of access to the electricity in the house, even if it means installing extra outlets. You begin to understand that you can talk to God, any time, day or night. You know that you only need to plug into the source: *pray!*

As construction continues, it gets somewhat confusing. The carpenter's there, the plumber's there, the furnace is being installed, insulation is going on, and drywall is being placed. The Lord shows you that He is not a God of confusion. He shows you His perspective on the construction, and He gives you His peace. Now you see that you have been learning the things of God from many people, along with His Word. According to 1 Corinthians 3:9, we are God's building!

There are some mishaps that hold up the construction: a crooked wall, the wrong flooring, cupboards that don't match, lighting in the wrong place, leaky plumbing. You think to yourself, *What is going on? Once I became a Christian, I thought it would be smooth sailing!* Then you discover that you have an enemy: Satan. He and his demonic forces do not want your Christian construction to be complete. Satan hopes you will give up and go back to your old ways. He messes with your mind by lying and deceiving and condemning you. If Satan had his way, he would knock down all the construction. But the house belongs to you, not the devil. You can tell him: "Get away from my house, in the name of Jesus. You have no right to be here. I belong to Jesus Christ!"

Construction continues, but there are messes to clean up. Trash must be hauled away. Our heavenly

Father knows how to help us, and He is willing when we ask Him. He throws the trash (sin) as far as the east is from the west and remembers it no more when we repent (Ps. 103:12).

Landscaping begins. The house looks more inviting. You realize that you have become more compassionate, kinder, and more merciful because of your trials. People see traits of Jesus in you. They are attracted to your newly painted home, your flowers, trees, and bushes (your more loving, more accepting personality).

You become a more mature Christian, but it does not end there. Upkeep lasts for the lifetime of the house. Philippians 2:13–15 says: "For it is God which worketh in you both to will and to do of His good pleasure. Do all things without murmurings and disputing; that ye may be blameless and harmless, the sons of God, without rebuke in the midst of a crooked and perverse nation, among whom ye shine as lights in the world."

Persecution, gossip, hatred, jealousy, and many other negative things may sit on your doorstep. You must learn to forgive in order to keep it clean. May the one who has begun a good work in you continue to perform it until you see Him face-to-face!

CHAPTER 20

TRUST IN THE LORD

After praise and worship, a group of us began to pray for someone who requested prayer. In my mind's eye, I saw a round spot on the person's tongue. I heard the word *bitter* in my mind. The impression I heard from the Lord was "This person is bitter and needs to repent." The person confessed a bitter situation and prayed for forgiveness. This person had been treated unfairly, but the Lord did not want bitterness to take root.

The bitterness was beginning to affect this person's personality and relationships. If we allow bitterness to take root, it will affect every aspect of our lives. Have you ever been around people who have allowed bitterness to take root in their lives? They have a negative attitude about life. They believe that everyone is against them. Deep-seated hurts and feelings of rejection can spawn resentment, bitterness, anger, and even hatred. If these things are not dealt with, we give the devil a mighty foothold. Only the Lord knows what is deep down in our hearts. Psalm 139:23 says, "Search me, O God, and know my heart: try me and know my thoughts: and see if there be any wicked way in me, and lead me in the way everlasting."

The Lord is merciful, gracious, kind, and slow to anger. He wants us all to repent of our sins and let Him work in our lives. We cannot measure His wisdom; it exceeds ours so greatly! He wants to talk to you and me. He wants to help us in our everyday lives. When we truly forgive, we are set free to receive His wise direction.

The Lord directs our paths. Psalm 37:23 says, "The steps of a *good* man are ordered by the Lord; and he delighteth in his way." Sometimes tough things happen in our lives that we do not understand. In Romans 8:28, God promises to take what seems bad and work it out for good. Ask Him to show you what good is coming out of your difficult situation.

Proverbs 3:7–14 says the following:

> Be not wise in thine own eyes; fear the Lord and depart from evil. It shall be health to thy navel and marrow to thy bones. Honour the Lord with thy substance and with the first-fruits of all thine increase: so shall thy barns be filled with plenty and thy presses shall burst out with new wine. My son, despise not the chastening of the Lord; neither be

weary of his correction: for whom the Lord loveth he correcteth; even as a father the son in whom he delighteth. Happy is the man that findeth wisdom, and the man that getteth understanding: for the merchandise of it is better than the merchandise of silver, and the gain thereof than fine gold.

Psalm 37 tells us to trust in the Lord, do good, delight ourselves in the Lord, rest in the Lord, wait patiently, do not fret because of evildoers, cease from anger, and forsake wrath. Verse 40 says, "And the Lord shall help them and deliver them: he shall deliver them from the wicked, and save them because they trust in him." We should learn to trust that the Lord will do what He says He will do! He wants us to ask and to trust.

CHAPTER 21

IRON AND CLAY

While I was seeking the Lord in prayer one day, the Lord put a vision in my mind, which I later shared with the home Bible study group. This vision was of a piece of stone made with iron and clay. God spoke to me in my mind and said, "You are living in the days of iron and clay." (This means the last of the last days.)

The Lord immediately moved my thoughts to the story of King Nebuchadnezzar in Daniel 2. The king had a dream of a great image. It was bright and magnificent. The image's head was composed of fine gold. The chest and arms were silver. His belly and thighs were brass, and the legs were made of iron. The feet and toes were a mixture of iron and clay. The king was very troubled during the night, but he could not remember the dream.

The only one who could tell the king the dream and interpret it was Daniel, who was one of the children of Israel. God had given Daniel and his three Israelite friends knowledge and skill in all learning and wisdom, and He gave Daniel understanding in all visions and dreams (Dan. 1:17). Daniel sought the Lord for the dream and interpretation. His three friends sought the Lord with him.

God gave Daniel the answer, and he relayed the dream to the king, along with the interpretation. He told the king that the gold represented his kingdom of Babylon. At that time, Babylon encompassed the entire known earth.

The silver represented a kingdom inferior to the king, which would arise after Babylon. The brass represented a third kingdom that would rule over all the known earth. The two iron legs would be the fourth kingdom, broken into two kingdoms. Then at the time of the end, there would be many kingdoms represented by the iron and clay. Verse 43 points out that these kingdoms would not be united, just as iron does not mix with clay.

Daniel 2:29 says, "As for thee, O king, thy thoughts came into thy mind upon thy bed, what should come to pass hereafter [in the future]; and he that revealeth secrets maketh known to thee what shall come to pass."

In the last part of the dream, a stone was cut without hands. The stone smote the image and broke it into pieces—the iron, clay, brass, silver, and gold. Then the stone became a great mountain and filled the whole earth (Dan. 2:34–35). This showed the king that the God of heaven would set up a kingdom that would never be destroyed. According to history, there have been enough empires to fulfill the dream of King Nebuchadnezzar, down to and including the iron and clay.

If we look at the nation of Israel, which came back to life in 1948, we can better understand the last days. The Lord said in Matthew 24:34, "Verily I say unto you, This generation shall not pass, till all these things be fulfilled." Matthew 24 is talking about the signs of the end times. Jesus said in verse 32 to "learn a parable of the fig tree." The fig tree represents Israel. We are to watch when the branch is yet tender and puts forth leaves. A new nation would have tender branches. We are told that when we see this, the time is near—even at the door!

Ezekiel 37 predicted that Israel would become a nation again. The Lord took Ezekiel, in the Spirit, to the valley of dry bones and told him to prophesy to the bones to rise again. In the Spirit, Ezekiel saw the bones produce flesh, and they stood up and formed a great army. The Lord showed Ezekiel that Israel would rise again. Israel did rise again in May of 1948. Ezekiel 36:24 says, "For I will take you from among the heathen, and gather you out of all countries, and will bring you into your own land." This is happening now!

Many pastors, prophets, evangelists, and others believe that the signs of the last days are now. I believe we will see the return of Jesus Christ in our lifetime. Watch for the signs of the end times: wars and rumors of wars, earthquakes increasing like birth pains, droughts (famines), pestilences, persecution for being a Christian, false prophets that lead many people astray, violence, immorality flourishing, people who are ever learning and never able to come to the knowledge of the truth. Second Timothy 3:2–5 says, "For men [and women] shall be lovers of their own selves, covetous, boasters, proud, blasphemers, disobedient to parents, unthankful unholy, without natural affection, trucebreakers, false accusers, incontinent [no self-control], fierce, despisers of those that are good, traitors, heady, highminded, lovers of pleasures more than lovers of God; having a form of godliness but denying the power thereof: from such turn away."

Daniel 12:4 speaks about the times of the end. It says that many shall run to and fro and knowledge shall be increased. People are traveling all over the world in all types of transportation. Knowledge is astonishing with everything at our fingertips through amazing technology.

The Lord wants us to watch for end-time signs because He wants you and me to live forever with Him. The Bible says the day of the Lord will come as a thief in the night. First Thessalonians 5:4–6 says: "But ye brethren are not in darkness, that the day should overtake you as a thief. Ye are all the children of light and the children of the day: we are not of the night, nor of darkness. Therefore let us not sleep, as do others; but let us watch and be sober."

CHAPTER 22

DARKNESS TO LIGHT

During my worship with other believers, the Lord put a vision in my mind. In the vision, I was in a room with a door that was open. It appeared that the open door led to a pitch-black room. I knew in my heart that the blackness represented evil, harm, sorrow, and immense problems. I could actually feel the fear and anxiety in my heart. I wanted to stay away from that black room!

When the Lord told me in the vision to walk through the blackness, I knew I had to obey. As I walked through in my mind, I discovered there was only a thin veil of black. The thin veil of darkness shows how Satan and demonic powers can lie and deceive us and give us the feeling of overwhelming hopelessness. These lies and deceptions heap guilt and fear on us and keep us from talking to God. We start looking at our lives from our distorted view instead of God's view.

On the other side of the veil were brightness and infinity with no walls. The Lord impressed on me that this represented His wisdom and His immeasurable hope in all of our life situations. When I shared this vision with the group, a couple shared that they were experiencing a lot of fear and confusion about a certain situation. This vision opened their eyes as to who was the cause. The realization helped them to be able to move forward into God's light and wisdom.

Colossians 1:13 says, we are "delivered from the power of darkness." When life seems hopeless, we must remember that we have a heavenly Father who can get us through. Demonic powers want to keep us in the dark. They do not want us to step through the veil that God opened for us at the cross. Jesus became sin in our place so that we could have eternal life and have access to the Father. God wants us to walk in His light.

In the Bible, Job experienced real darkness. He lost his wealth, his ten children, and his health after the Lord removed the hedge of protection against the devil's attacks. The Lord allowed this in order to test Job's faith. Satan challenged God by saying that Job was a worshiper only because he had been extremely blessed by God. He was enormously wealthy and greatly honored in the community. Job's friends criticized him and tried to blame him for what he was experiencing. They thought that Job had certainly brought all the gloom upon himself.

Emotions were plentiful. Maybe you can relate to some of the emotions Job experienced. When Job was told by his last four living servants that all his wealth and his ten children were gone, he believed that God had taken it all away. He tore his robe in grief but still worshiped God. He knew God had given him everything and said that God had a right to take it away. When Satan struck his entire body with boils, Job's wife told him to curse God and die. The Bible says that he still did not sin with his lips.

Job's emotions included grief, sorrow he had ever been born, no peace, feeling faint, discouragement, fearfulness (he admitted that he always feared that everything would be taken away), hopelessness, wanting to die, overwhelmed, and unable to sleep. He experienced spiritual anguish *(Why me, Lord?)*, bitterness, fear and terror through the night, perplexity, feeling attacked unjustly, feeling innocent, knowing that he had always trusted God but was not getting answers from God, weariness, confusion, and mockery of his faith *(Where is God now?)*. Job suffered defensiveness, criticism from close friends, wanting to hide, feeling comfortless, no confidence, feeling like he was in darkness, crying, feeling totally alone, thinking God hated him, and desertion by family and friends (hurt). Job had a deep sense of feeling persecuted, bemoaning his wealthy years that had turned to poverty, mourning that he had helped the poor when he had wealth but evil came upon him anyway, and irritation that the wicked prospered. Job was sitting in that thin black veil of satanic deceit!

During these emotional months, Job tried to think about God. He said he knew that his Redeemer lived, and even after his body was destroyed, he would see God (Job 19:25–26). He began to understand that wisdom comes only from God.

Job took the counsel of friends. The friends did not have the knowledge to counsel correctly. They were trying to counsel without talking to God. They were positive that Job had some kind of secret sin and God was punishing him. But Job was persecuted by Satan, not God!

Job learned that God is sovereign and His ways are always wise, no matter what. In the midst of Job's helplessness, God allowed him to recognize his pride and self-righteousness when He spoke to Job from a whirlwind. Job was sorry and repented for blaming God for his situation. He learned to truly trust God.

Job prayed for his friends. After that the Lord blessed Job by giving him twice as much as he had in the beginning. We can learn from the book of Job. When Satan covers our paths with a dark veil, we should say: "Lord, I trust you to teach me in this difficult situation; please take what Satan thinks is for evil and bring good out of this. Help me, Lord; I need your perfect wisdom."

It was important in the eyes of the Lord for Job to forgive and pray for his friends. Job 42:10 says, "And the Lord turned the captivity of Job when he prayed for his friends." Job was set free from Satan's bondage and was free to receive from God. All his brothers, sisters, friends, and acquaintances came and ate with Job and gave him strong comfort. Job

42:11 says, "Every man also gave him a piece of his money and everyone an earring of gold."

Do you know people who are going through difficult and stressful situations? They may be standing in the dark veil of defeat. It may be you standing in that dark veil. Remember that God is for you, not against you, and very capable and willing to help you. Reach out to Jesus with thanksgiving and honor, and let your requests be known to Him. He does not want you to stay in the darkness; He wants you to move into His glorious light. Learn what Job learned: God is all powerful, awesome, and perfectly capable of taking care of you in any situation!

CHAPTER 23

TRAPPED

As I was communing with the Lord during worship, I saw a vision of a folding type of paper fan with wooden sticks separating the sections. The sticks were obviously a part of the fan and could not be moved. My impression from the Lord was that the sticks represented people.

One stick was green (I knew it meant living). Then I saw a vine growing from the top of the living stick. The vine was producing fruit and growing onto various kinds of trees. The Lord impressed on me that the trees also represented people. In my mind, I heard the Lord say: "You may feel trapped in your situation, but I can cause fruit to grow and you will grow out from this trapped situation as you seek Me. The size of the fan [or trapped situation] will decrease as you do My will and reach out to others."

I shared this with the group to encourage them that nothing, absolutely nothing, is too difficult for God. He just wants us to listen to Him and obey Him. He wants us to share the eternal life-giving gospel of Jesus Christ.

The emotion of being trapped can cause you to feel resentment, bitterness, anger, sadness, discouragement, fear, devastation, and many other negative emotions. Trapped can be minor or major, dreadful or devastating. It can cause a little anxiety, a complete breakdown, or anything in between. It is where you can't get past your situation or your overwhelming emotions.

Your life may be going along smoothly, and then suddenly you are ambushed or caught totally unaware. It's an uncomfortable place. Sometimes you can barely function in an emotionally trapped situation. You may go through the motion of living, but with no joy or peace. Maybe you want to pray but do not know how or even where to start.

Jesus told the disciples to wait until He sent the Holy Spirit. He said that the Holy Spirit would help them. When Jesus walked on the earth, He was in a fleshly body and could be in only one place at one time. When He ascended into heaven, He was then unrestrained from the flesh and able to send the Holy Spirit.

Jesus is the Father and the Son and the Holy Spirit (1 John 5:7). If you want Him to, He will lavish the Holy Spirit on you (Acts 2:39). As I've stated before, if you ask, He will baptize you in the Holy Spirit. Acts 1:5 says, "For John truly baptized with water, but ye shall be baptized with the Holy Ghost not many days hence." God chose a day to pour out His Holy Spirit when people from all areas of the Roman Empire would be in Jerusalem. There were people from Italy, Greece, Egypt, Asia, and all the areas in between. The day was called Pentecost, a Jewish religious holiday held after the barley harvest.

The Lord knew that the city would be filled with people speaking many different languages. During that special time, there were 120 people meeting in an upper room to pray and wait for the Holy Spirit to be sent to them, just as Jesus had promised them. Among the 120 were the disciples; Mary, the mother of Jesus; other women; and the brothers of Jesus (Acts 1:12–15). Acts 2:1–8 says:

> And when the day of Pentecost was fully come, they were all with one accord in one place. And suddenly there came a sound from heaven as of a rushing mighty wind, and it filled all the house where they were sitting. And there appeared unto them cloven tongues like as of fire, and it sat upon each of them. And they were all filled with the Holy Ghost and began to speak with other tongues, as the Spirit gave them utterance. And there were dwelling at Jerusalem Jews, devout men, out of every nation under heaven. Now when this was noised abroad, the multitude came together, and were confounded because that every man heard them speak in his own language. And they were all amazed and

marveled, saying one to another, Behold, are not all these which speak Galileans? And how hear we every man in our own tongue, wherein we were born?

They were all filled with the Holy Spirit and spoke in languages they had not learned. The Spirit gave them the words to speak! On that day, 3,000 people were baptized and filled with the Holy Spirit and spoke in languages given to them by the Lord. Jude, verse 20, says, "But ye, beloved, building up yourselves on your most holy faith, praying in the Holy Ghost." First Corinthians 14:4 tells us that when we speak in an unknown (to us) language, we edify (or build up or encourage) ourselves. Romans 8:26–27 tells us that we do not know what we should pray for, but the Spirit makes intercession for us according to the will of God.

There is fruit that is produced when you are filled with the Holy Spirit and walking in the Spirit. Walking in the Spirit (listening to and talking to the Lord) is essential. The Bible says in Galations 5:22-23, "<u>But the fruit of the Spirit is love, joy</u>, peace, long-suffering [patience], gentleness, goodness, faith, meekness [honoring God], temperance: against such there is no law."

When you go through an unbearable time, you may need more than your own intellect to give you peace and direction. We live in a volatile and unpredictable world. We have at our disposal a heavenly language (tongue) that we can pray in when we do not know what to pray. It completely bypasses the intellect so that the Holy Spirit prays the perfect prayer. We think we know what to pray, but sometimes we pray amiss (James 4:3). The Lord wants to help us even in knowing what to pray.

As you trust, obey, and pray in the Spirit, you can be lifted out of the trapped situation. Many times the Lord will give you Scriptures from His Word to encourage you.

Many years ago when the sins of some well-known Christians were exposed, I remember what the Lord said to me, after I prayed in my heavenly language. He said, "If you think I'm this hard on the Christians, how hard do you think I will be on the non-Christians?" Later I discovered He was giving me His words from 1 Peter 4:17–18: "For the time *is come* that judgment must *begin* at the house of God: and if it first begin at us, what shall the end be of them that obey not the gospel of God? And if the righteous scarcely be saved, where shall the ungodly and the sinner appear?"

Another time I was praying in my heavenly language because I didn't know how to pray for a person who was terribly backslidden. After I prayed, the Lord said in my mind: "He is like the prodigal son. He was once in the Father's house but chose to go his own way. But... *he will come back!*" (He did come back to the Lord three years later.) The prodigal son story is found in Luke 15:11–32.

Jesus wants you to understand things from His perspective. Don't walk in the vanity of your own mind, having the understanding darkened (Eph. 4:17–18). If you are feeling trapped, give Him a chance to lift you up and give you His strong peace and comfort.

CHAPTER 24

DEAD WOOD

In this vision during worship, I saw a row of wooden shacks with the wind of the Holy Spirit blowing across them. My impression from the Lord was that the shacks represented people. A closer look showed gorgeous green buds growing out of the dead wood of the shacks. The greenery contained flowers and was exquisite. The impression the Lord gave me was "Without Jesus, we can do nothing; we are like dead wood." Jesus wants to give you new life. He wants to take what looks dead and make it beautiful and full of life. As always, I shared this with the church group.

Moses led the Israelites out of their bondage in Egypt. He led them into the wilderness where they wandered for forty years. The people experienced many miracles during those years, but they still chose to whine and complain and rebel. The Lord dealt with them during every rebellion. Many times they did not truly believe that God had chosen Moses and Aaron to be the leaders. They were prideful and jealous.

In Numbers 17, the Lord spoke to Moses and gave him specific instructions. Each leader of the twelve tribes was told to bring his own wooden rod to Moses. The Lord told Moses to write each man's name upon his own rod and to also write Aaron's name upon the rod of the tribe of Levi. Moses took the twelve rods with names and put them in the tabernacle before the testimony in obedience to God. I'm sure they were lined up like dead wood. The Lord said in Numbers 17:5, "And it shall come to pass *that* the man's rod, whom I shall choose, shall blossom; and I will make to cease from me the murmurings of the children of Israel, whereby they murmur against you."

The next day Moses went into the tabernacle, and one rod immediately grabbed his attention. Aaron's rod contained buds and also blossoms and even yielded ripe almonds, all at the same time! There was no doubt that God had chosen Aaron as priest.

Those twelve rods were all dead wood, but God demonstrated His majesty and awesome power when He chose to bring Aaron's rod back to life. We were all dead in our sins, but when we accepted Christ, He made us come alive!

You may feel like dead wood. You may be a backslidden Christian or not even a believer. Regardless, the Lord can make you alive eternally and help you to blossom and produce fruit. The Bible promises that the righteous will flourish like palm trees and will produce fruit even in old age (Ps. 92:12–14). You can produce fruit when you tell other generations about the strength and power of the Lord and how He has been faithful to you. Producing fruit is when you help others to believe. Ask the Lord to take your dead wood and inject His life into you. He wants you to flourish. Do you feel the wind of the Holy Spirit? God has chosen you!

CHAPTER 25

SEATED IN HEAVENLY PLACES

The Lord gave me a vision of us worshiping in the clouds. In my mind, He said, "You are all seated in heavenly places with Jesus Christ right now!" I shared this with the church group. The Lord gave me his words out of Ephesians 2:4–6: "But God, who is rich in mercy, for his great love, wherewith he loved us, even when we were dead in sins hath quickened us [made us alive] together with Christ, (by grace ye are saved;) and hath raised us up together, and made us sit together in heavenly places in Christ Jesus." He wants us to be near Him.

Another time there was a wonderful awe of God during our worship. The Lord presented me with a vision of angels standing behind each one of us. They were worshiping God with us. I could not see them perfectly; it was more like a spiritual apparition. However, I was very aware of their presence. We were all engulfed in the holiness of God. In the vision, the walls in the room had disappeared. We all felt like we were in a heavenly place.

Many good books have been written about angels, so I won't go into any great detail here. Psalm 103:20 says, "Bless the Lord, ye his angels, that excel in strength, that do his commandments, hearkening unto the voice of his word." In Luke 15:10, Jesus says, "Likewise, I say unto you, there is joy in the presence of the angels of God over one sinner that repenteth." Psalm 148:2, 5 says, "Praise ye him all his angels.... Let them praise the name of the Lord: for he commanded and they were created." Hebrews 13:2 says, "Be not forgetful to entertain strangers: for thereby some have entertained angels unawares."

It is so comforting to be in communication with our heavenly Father. He wants to communicate with you! Spiritually, you can be right there with Him in heavenly places. Many years ago when we were moving from one state to another and praying that the Lord would lead us to the house where He wanted us to live, I prayed this prayer: "Dear Lord, thank you so much that You care about our lives. You care so much that You died for us in order that we might have eternal life. I know that You have a plan for us and You are directing our path. Please help us find the house that You want us to have. As a matter of fact, Lord, You already know where we will live. You could show the house to me. Please show me what the house looks like."

As I continued to worship the Lord, a vision popped into my mind. I saw the bottom part of a house with double brown doors in the front. I saw a circular road in front, like a court. Circling around the court was a very light jade-colored car.

My husband was already working in the new state and had narrowed our home search to about fifteen houses. I did not tell him about the vision. After we had spent two exhausting days looking at homes, our realtor turned into a court and pulled up to a home with double brown entrance doors. In my spirit, I knew that was the house! I felt like I was going to burst. I wanted to say, "That's it!"

I kept quiet about the vision because I wanted Tom to choose the house as a confirmation that I really did hear from the Lord. He liked the house and asked me if we should make an offer. That's when I told him about the vision. Several weeks later, after we had finally moved into the house with our three children, Tom came home with a company car that had been assigned to him. It was light jade in color!

The Lord wants to be involved in your everyday life. Talk to Him. Share your deepest desires and concerns with Him. He loves you!

CHAPTER 26

ARE YOU READY?

In this vision during worship, we were all in a boat that was gently floating down the river. Harsh waves came against the gentle flow, but they could not cut through and cause harm to us or the boat. The understanding the Lord gave me was that we were to stay in the boat, which represented Jesus Christ, who is our safety. The gentle flowing water was the Holy Spirit.

The Lord wants you to trust Him with every part of your life. He really is interested in you and wants to help you.

While worshiping another time, I had a vision of a large expensive boat. The Lord said in my mind, "Get in the boat and I will take you out into the deep—you won't drown!" As always, I shared this with the Bible home group. The Lord gave His special encouragement by saying, "You won't drown." Going out into the deep is the place where you must totally depend on the Lord. It is the place where you must trust and obey.

If you want to move forward in your spiritual walk, it is important to get into the boat of Jesus Christ and let Him take you where He knows you need to go. Jesus is saying: "Will you trust Me? Will you believe Me? Will you go with Me?"

We live in a very selfish society with a "me first" attitude. The Lord wants us to put Him first. He put us first when He died for us. God deserves to be put first in our lives. He is not a man; He is God. He came in the form of a man for our salvation. Now we can relate to Him.

Many biblical Scriptures relate the characteristics of God. According to Scripture, some of God's distinctive characteristics are as follows: companion and friend, wants us to come to Him, will not let the righteous be moved, wants us to seek Him and believe, makes all things possible, controls power and might, keeps His promises, gives good things, gives victory, sustains us, keeps watch over us, rejoices over us, righteous, gives wisdom, gives richly, always consistent, binds up wounds, mansion builder, fulfills, and dwells within us. He lets us use His name (Jesus), freely sends the Comforter (Holy Spirit), engraves us on His palms, satisfies, heals broken hearts, examines our deepest motives, rules with discretion, will not accuse us, truly cares about us, searches all hearts, and wants to be known. In addition, His nature is holy, slow to anger, remembers us, compassionate, will not reject us, leads us, gives faith, rescues, overflowing kindness, guards us, orders our steps, will not forsake us, comforts us, merciful, provides, will not scold us for asking, provides justice and truth, a very present helper, upholds us with His victorious right hand, and will not come to us in wrath. God suffered and died for us. He rewards us and gives us a lighted path. Other traits are trustworthy, a strong tower, blesses us, heals, all-powerful, gives rest and peace and hope, wants us to abide in Him, wants us to talk to Him (listener), will not disappoint us, takes our worries (burden bearer), sets us free from sin (saves us), freely pardons, while in the flesh resisted temptation, delights in us, loves us unconditionally, gracious, teaches, gives us joy and songs, and protector (refuge). Besides all of these characteristics, God gives confidence, answers us, reveals Himself to obedient ones, delivers us, lovingly guides us, forgives, waits for us, gives freely, works for our good, hides us in Him, gives strength, understands us, knows us, and is always with us. Furthermore He is rich in love, faithful, organized, sinless, spotless, pure, honest, and fair. The Lord God is the creator, priest, and king, and He takes the sting out of death, destroys the works of the devil, and gives eternal life. He loves you and me and wants to talk to you and me! God should be honored with worship and praise. I am sure that others could add many more traits because the list is unlimited.

Are you ready? Do you want to follow the one who wants to talk to you? If yes, then the following is a prayer for you to pray:

Dear Lord, I believe that You came to this earth, in the flesh, in order to die for my sins. Please forgive me for my sins and wash me as white as snow. Please come into my heart and into my life. I thank You that I am now a born-again Christian. I praise You for all You have done for me! Please fill me with Your Holy Spirit—saturate me. Please fill my mouth with a heavenly language that I can pray to bypass my intellect. I need to be built up and encouraged by Your Holy Spirit. Please become Lord of my life and help me to be what You want me to be. Please lead me to a church where I can learn more about You. I thank You! In the name of Jesus Christ, amen!

Welcome to the eternal family of God. Heaven and eternity are now your destiny!

Some of you may already be Christian and just need a power surge in your spiritual circuit.

I pray for everyone who reads this book that the Lord will bless you mightily and give you His strong encouragement!

First John 5:11–13 (emphasis added): "And this is the record, that God hath given to us eternal life and this life is in his Son. He that hath the Son hath life; *and* he that hath not the Son of God hath not life. These things have I written unto you that believe on the name of the Son of God; *that ye may know that ye have eternal life,* and that ye may believe on the name of the Son of God."